PIANO SOLO

BILL EVANS

19 Arrangements for Solo Piano

Cover photo: Louis Ouzer

ISBN 978-0-634-01872-5

EXCLUSIVELY DISTRIBUTED BY

Visit Hal Leonard Online at
www.halleonard.com

Contact us:
Hal Leonard
7777 West Bluemound Road
Milwaukee, WI 53213
Email: info@halleonard.com

In Europe, contact:
Hal Leonard Europe Limited
42 Wigmore Street
Marylebone, London, W1U 2RN
Email: info@halleonardeurope.com

In Australia, contact:
Hal Leonard Australia Pty. Ltd.
4 Lentara Court
Cheltenham, Victoria, 3192 Australia
Email: info@halleonard.com.au

Re: Person I Knew

Bill Evans was one of the great jazz improvisers of the Twentieth Century. It is no surprise there-fore that his compositional skills were equally impressive, because composing is improvising in slow motion. This is not to say that all great improvisers are great composers as well. It seems that the best jazz composers are comfortable with keyboard harmony, whether they are pianists or not, as demonstrated by Miles Davis, Wayne Shorter, Thelonious Monk, Duke Ellington, John Coltrane, Tadd Dameron, John Abercrombie, Bud Powell, Jerry Bergonzi, Chick Corea, Dave Samuels, Herbie Hancock and many others. Another important element is that of developing one's given tal-ents and abilities. Bill was born with a great talent, but his was no "Bonsai Talent," that is, one which is present but remains small and is never developed. Bill worked long and hard putting the puzzle of music together. In his own words, "I had to work very hard to take things apart. I had to build my whole musical style. ...Because I had to build it so meticulously, I think it worked out bet-ter in the end, because it gave me a complete understanding of everything I was doing." This hard work was reflected in the fact that early on he enrolled as a graduate student in composition at New York's Mannes School of Music. His time studying was well spent, as confirmed by his compo-sitional output. Of his time at Mannes, Bill said "When I got out of the Army in 1954 I went back and did three semesters of post-graduate composition work at Mannes College in New York City, and the work and assignments that I was doing then fell into an entirely different idiom than the idiom I play in. I think the reason is obvious—when you're improvising you must be able to move and to handle a certain area, whereas when you compose you can take a week to write three meas-ures if necessary, so you can reach for areas of music that you ordinarily couldn't handle in a spontaneous way."

The lyricism, emotionality, tension and release which earmarked his playing, are also evident in his compositions, which served in large part as vehicles for his improvisations. Certainly Bill's harmonic knowledge and depth are reflected in his writing. However, when asked how he puts tunes togeth-er, he replied, "I've written a lot of different ways. At one period of my life I had a manuscript book that I carried with me everywhere. I wanted to get away from the patterns that writing at the piano might influence me into. I went all the way back to whole-note melodies and half-note melodies, basically on the pentatonic scale, trying to get back to the fundamentals of melodic structure. When I write away from the piano I don't think about harmony at all, and sometimes later I'm amazed at the harmonies that a melody will imply. I've written things at the piano, I've written one thing where I wrote the harmony first and then the melody, I've written things that came easy and things that I just had to sit there and take it apart and screw it back together and saw it in half, and finally end up with something that sounds like it's natural. I have notebooks filled with 12-tone rows and so forth. When I didn't feel like thinking music, I would use that as a sort of mental exercise. The peculiar thing about it is, I did a lot of that, and I don't think it has contributed anything to my musical thinking. There just doesn't seem to be anything natural in it as far as it relates to me. Well, I've made a couple of little tunes out of rows, but that's all."

One can hear a couple of important factors in this answer. The continuous work and many approaches to writing, which were in fact major parts of Bill's musical persona, and the sincere hum-bleness in his attitude. I witnessed this first hand when I was playing with Stan Getz in the fall of 1979. Bill's trio and Stan's quartet did a tour of Europe, many of the gigs were double bills, with the Evans trio opening for the Getz group. During the days, we traveled on planes together. Bill was into taping his performance each night, as he was working on developing melodic and rhythmic displacement in his R.H. lines. Many times he played tapes for me, pointing out where he was try-ing to implement this displacement, commenting that he didn't really achieve his goal. As far as I was concerned, I thought it all sounded great! But of course I always felt that about Bill's music. The first time we met was when Bill was playing at New York's Village Vanguard, where I somehow sum-moned up the courage to speak to him, resulting in several lessons at his apartment in the Bronx, (free of charge, unheard of today) with us playing four hands on his Chickering baby grand piano.

It was there that I got to experience, in a more visceral way, his amazing harmonic sense, which he not only played, but spoke about. The concept of traveling down many different "avenues" to reach a harmonic goal stuck with me, and influenced much of my own playing and writing.

These concepts are found throughout Bill's compositions, along with many of the harmonic colors he was so fond of. A liberal use of half-diminished chords, a product of melodic minor scale harmony, is a dark sound, highly emotional. Thick dominant seventh chords (and its cousin, the diminished seventh chord) many times altered with ♯9's and Bill's favorite ♯5's abound, which give these tunes a great sense of motion. Bill was one of the first jazz composers to use the major 7 ♯5 sound, which is also related to melodic minor scale harmony. Along with these dark, thick, and dissonant sounds, Bill loved the prettier notes as well, as in the minor 11th chords, and the dominant seventh sus 4 chords. The use of modal harmonies is well documented, as in Dorian, Mixolydian, Phrygian, and Lydian modes over longer harmonic rhythms. And the brightest sound, the major seventh chord is used to great effect to balance out the more tense sounds, and provide a platform for harmonic release.

Thanks to his exhaustive knowledge of standard tunes, Bill had a strong appreciation for form in composition, as is evidenced in many of his tunes. Along with, or as part of this awareness of form, melodic and rhythmic development play equally important roles. All these components result in a wide variety of tunes, of which nineteen are presented in this collection. The goal of this volume is to provide some of the classic Evans compositions in a player friendly form. If you're a pianist, of any level or ability, or even if piano is not your main instrument, the tunes presented here are arranged to be easy to play, with a minimum of intervallic stretches, simplified voicings, and where necessary, simplified rhythms—all the while keeping in mind the original intent, style, and sound of Bill Evans. Many of the devices Bill used are present in these arrangements. L.H. shell voicings (two or three notes, usually the third and seventh of the chord, aka: guide tones, along with the root.) The R.H. contains the melody, which oftentimes is harmonized. Some of the ways this is accomplished are; triads—major or minor with the melody note on top, four-way close voicings, and its offshoot, drop-two voicings (taking the note second from the top in a four-way close voicing, and dropping it down one octave.) Occasionally a rootless voicing is played by the L.H. These are voicings without roots, which contain more of the chord extensions, i.e. 9, 11, 13, which Bill developed in the late fifties–early sixties, one of his major contributions to changing the soundscape and function of jazz piano. Bill was also fond of bass pedal points, a static bass note over which the harmony changes. As you read through the tunes, you will begin to recognize many of these techniques. Bill would be thrilled to know that from here, you would be able to arrange and write tunes of your own, using these ideas as jumping off points to express your musical thoughts.

Some personal observations about Bill's tunes:

I have recorded many of these tunes on various projects of my own, some more than once, as Bill was known to do himself. One that rises above all others for me is "Turn Out The Stars," certainly one of the most evocative compositions in the collection. Originally written as part of a four part suite in honor of his father, Bill recorded this tune many times, most notably as a solo on the *Town Hall Concert*, and in duet with Jim Hall on *Intermodulation*. My first recording of this tune was also a duet, with guitarist John Abercrombie. As John put it so well, "This tune is so well constructed, it plays itself." Another personal favorite is "Waltz For Debby" (truly Bill's hit tune!), probably his best known work. With its singable, memorable melody, and deceptively simple harmonies, this is a tune that stays with you. Some of my other favorites are "Peri's Scope," "Orbit," "Laurie," "Very Early" and "Time Remembered," all of which I have recorded. Another significant tune is "Your Story," which I recorded on the *Bill Evans Tribute Album*. I had never heard Bill play it, and had only his original lead sheet from which to draw. This was ironically Bill's last composition. Perhaps the centerpiece of the collection for me, is "Peace Piece," which appears on the CD *Everybody Digs Bill Evans*. Recorded Dec. 15, 1958, from serene, pastoral passages to Messiaenic birdcalls, it transcends music via nature, and sets the tone for improvisations to come. As Bill described it, "I was going to use that ostinato bass as an introduction to Leonard Bernstein's tune 'Some Other Time,' which if you've ever heard it has the same bass figure, except that it changes when the harmony changes. What happened was that I started to play the introduction, and it started to get so much of its own feeling and identity that I figured, well, I'll keep going." Bill states further, "I don't think that essentially it is any different in feeling than what I do, but stylistically it would appear to be, because it's almost classical in its approach." The arrangement here has taken all the notes played on the original recording, and simplified them rhythmically. This piece is played rubato, and can be freely interpreted. A sampling of the original recording will help you to realize your own version. Of course this goes for all the tunes, listening to Bill's versions can serve as a guide to how you might like to approach playing them. You'll notice that two tunes are presented in two keys, "For Nenette," and "My Bells." The original keys are Db major and B major respectively. During my "field test" (thanks to Charlie Freeman), I became aware that even given the pared down arrangements, these tunes were difficult to read through. A decision was made to transpose them to easier, more commonly played keys, but I felt it important to have them in the original keys as well. This not only gives one an appreciation for Bill's technical prowess, but also points out his sensitivity to the timbre and resonance of tonal centers.

One other note of irony, after all the nights of listening to Bill live at the Vanguard, and the Top of the Gate, both in NYC, I got a call on September 11, 1980 to sub for him at Fat Tuesdays, also in NYC. For four nights I was the pianist in the Bill Evans trio. From that exhilaration and elation, the following day turned to shock and sadness upon the news of Bill's passing. Thanks to his prolific composing abilities, his music lives on for us to enjoy. The tunes in this book are in a dormant state, it's up to you to bring them to life.

Andy LaVerne
June, 2000

About Andy LaVerne

Jazz pianist, composer, and arranger Andy LaVerne studied at Juilliard, Berklee, and the New England Conservatory, and took private lessons from pianist Bill Evans. The list of musicians with whom LaVerne has worked reads like a Who's Who in jazz: Frank Sinatra, Stan Getz, Woody Herman, Dizzy Gillespie, Chick Corea, Lionel Hampton, Michael Brecker, Elvin Jones, and numerous others. A prolific recording artist, his projects as a leader number over 40, among the most recent is a quartet recording featuring trumpeter Randy Brecker, bassist George Mraz, and drummer Al Foster, *Four Miles*, which reached the top ten on the Gavin Jazz Chart.

LaVerne is also a prominent jazz educator, having released a series of instructional videos, *Guide to Modern Jazz Piano, Vols. 1 & 2*, and *Jazz Piano Standards* (Homespun Tapes), featuring the Yamaha Disklavier, as well as the video, *In Concert* (Homespun), with John Abercrombie. He is the author of *Handbook of Chord Substitutions, Tons of Runs* (Ekay). *The Music Of Andy LaVerne* (SteepleChase Publications) has just been published. *Countdown To Giant Steps* (Aebersold Jazz) is a two CD play-a-long with companion book, of which LaVerne served as player/producer/writer. *Tunes You Thought You Knew* (Aebersold Jazz) is a LaVerne play-a-long CD/book set.

Andy is the recipient of five Jazz Fellowships from the National Endowment for the Arts. He has appeared at concerts, festivals, and clubs throughout the world, and has also given clinics at universities, colleges, and conservatories around the world. LaVerne is professor of Jazz Piano at The Hartt School, The University of Hartford.

Bill's Hit Tune

Music by BILL EVANS

Medium Swing

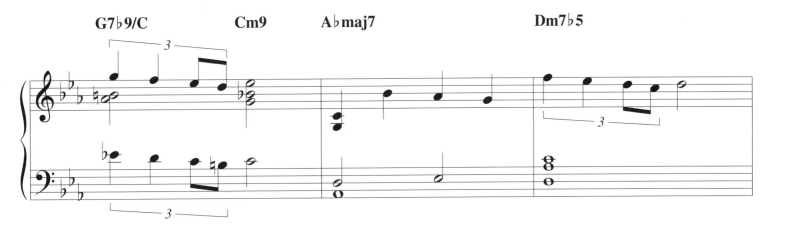

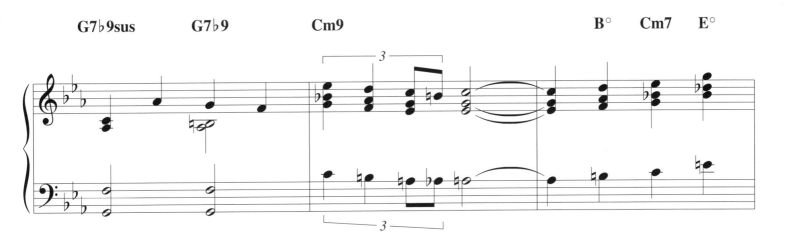

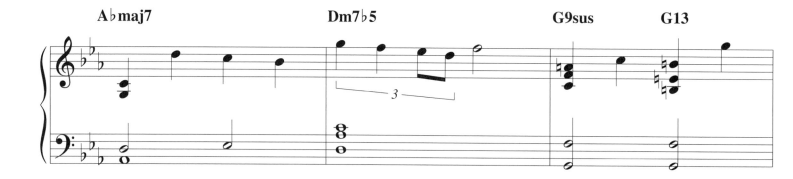

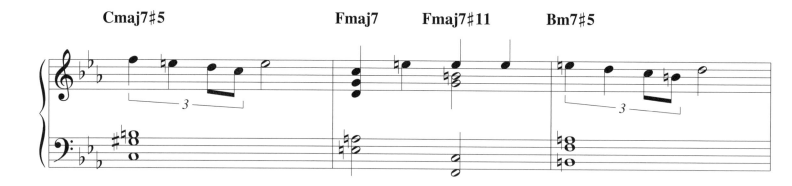

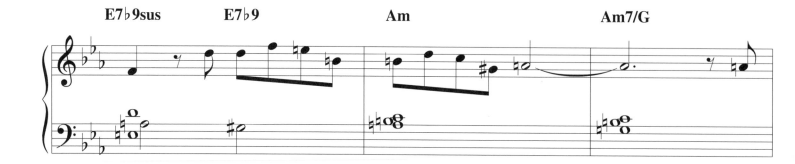

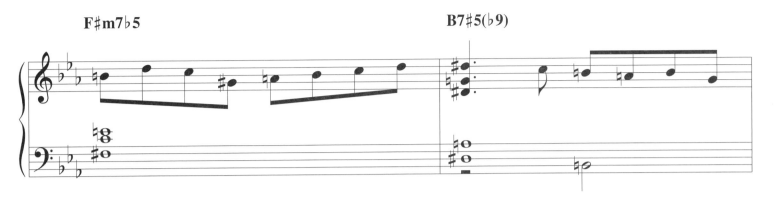

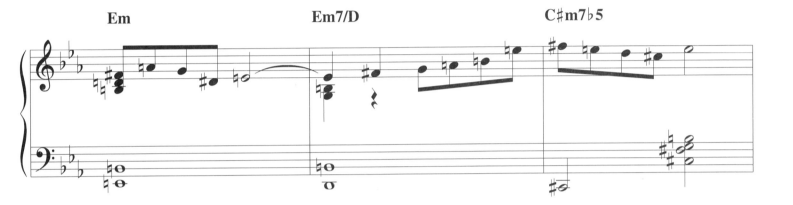

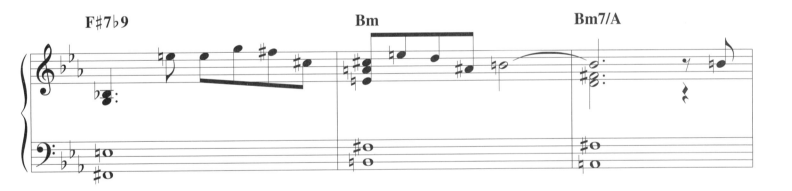

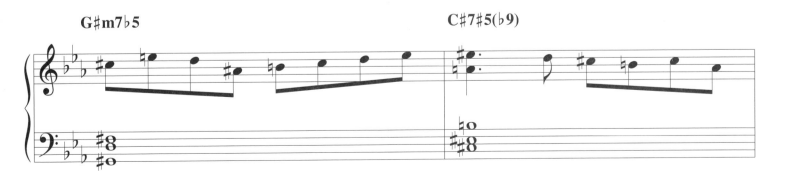

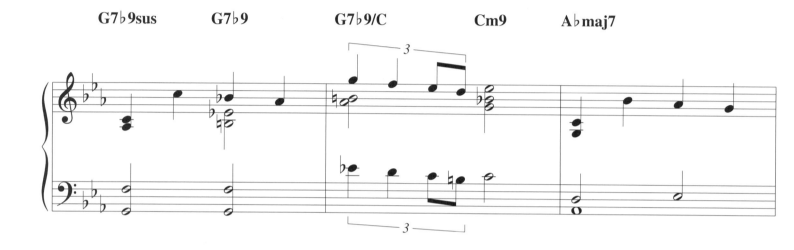

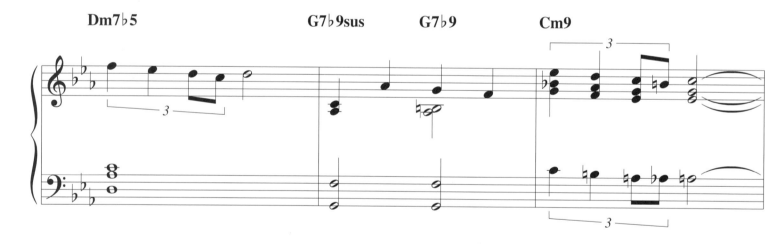

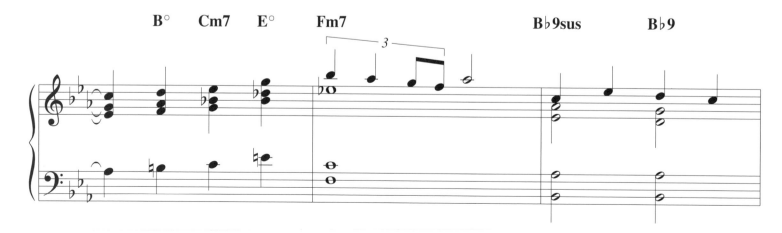

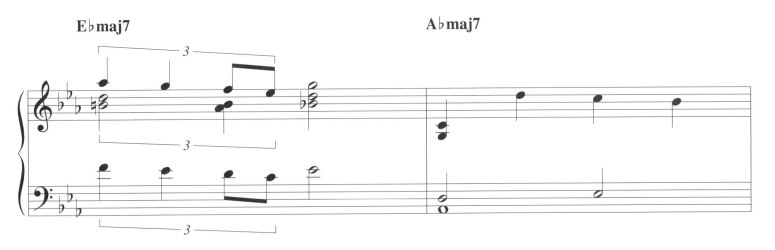

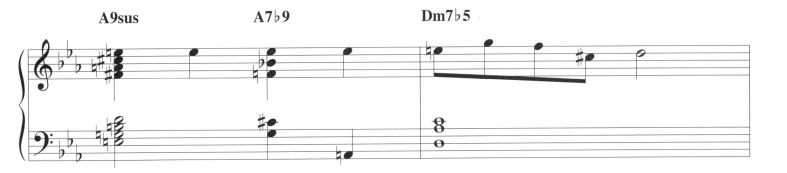

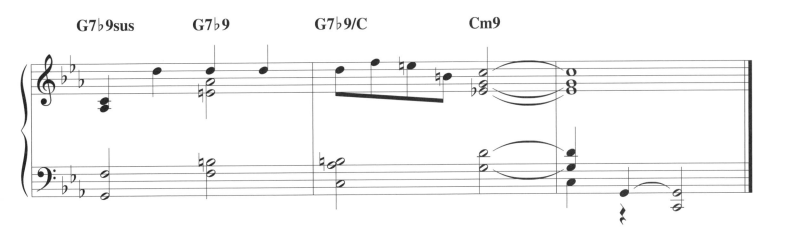

Children's Play Song

Music by BILL EVANS

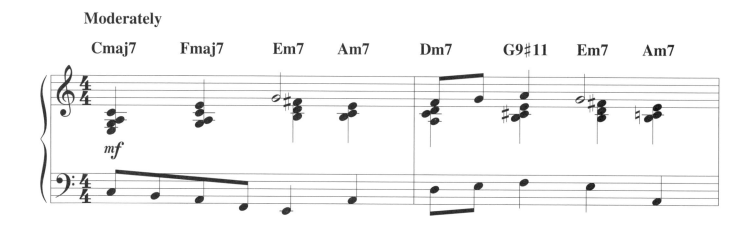

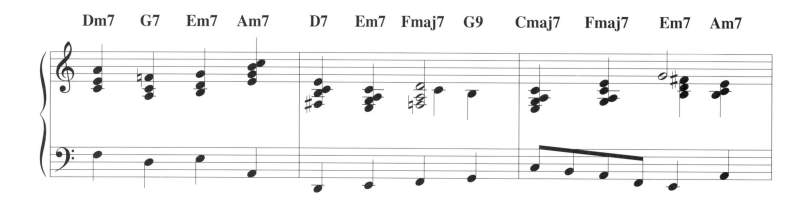

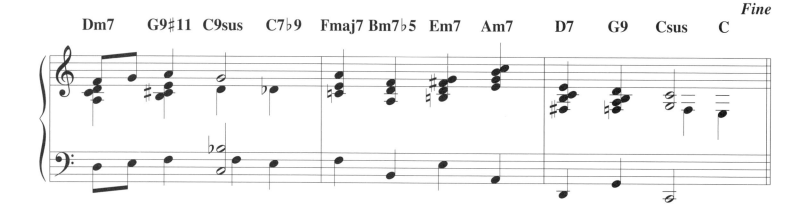

G7sus

D.C. al Fine

For Nenette

(C)

Music by BILL EVANS

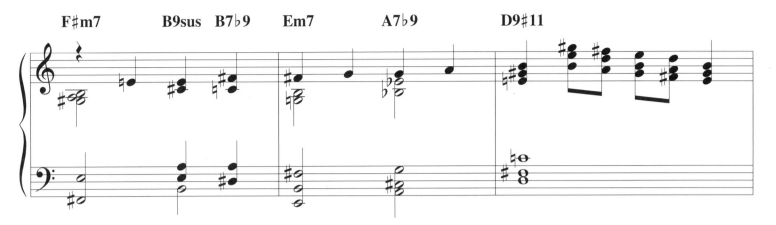

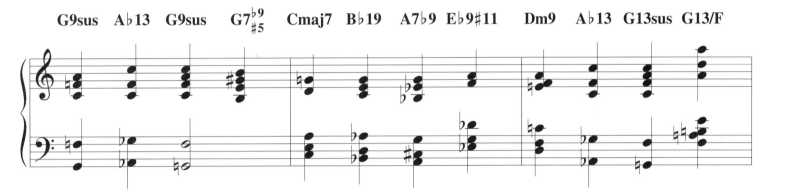

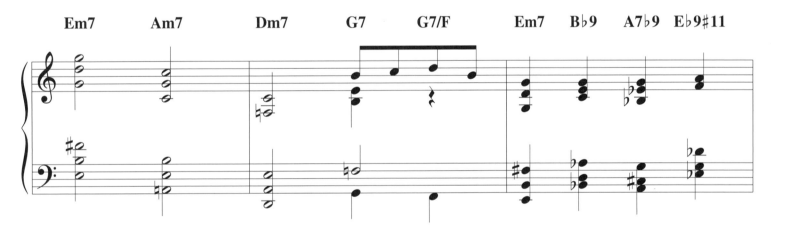

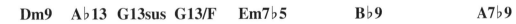

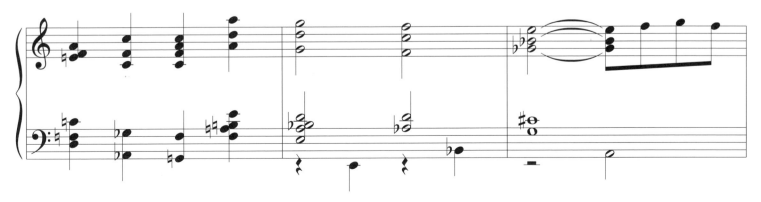

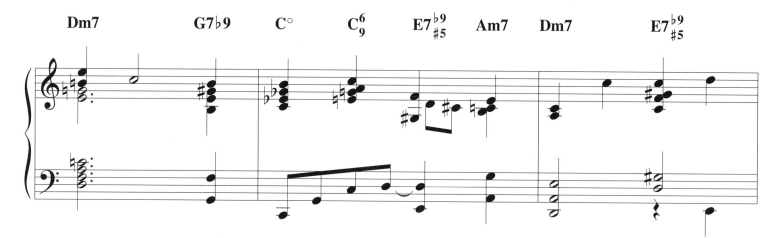

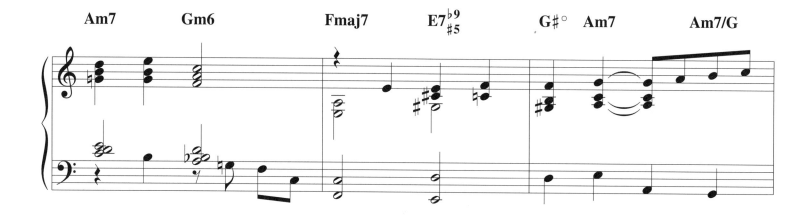

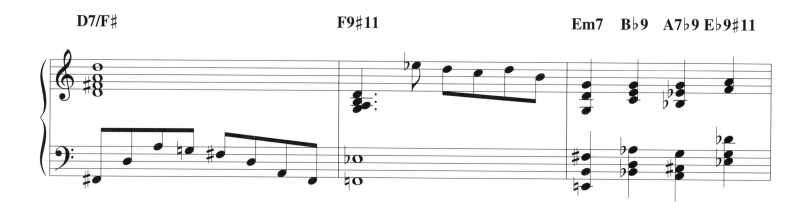

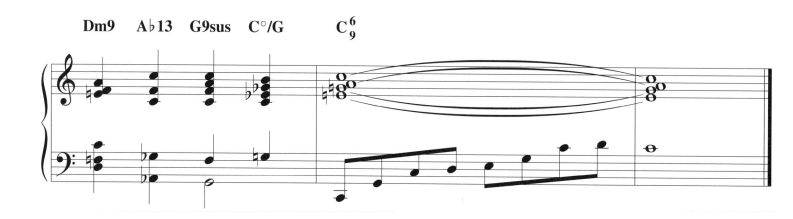

For Nenette
(D♭)

Music by BILL EVANS

Ballad Tempo

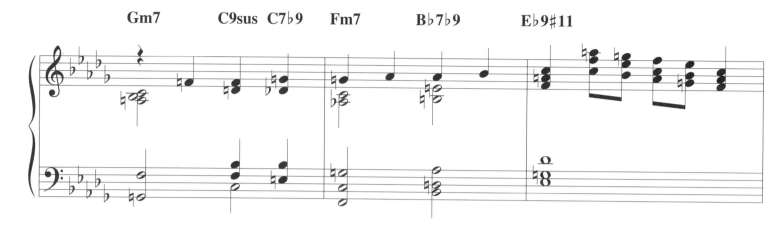

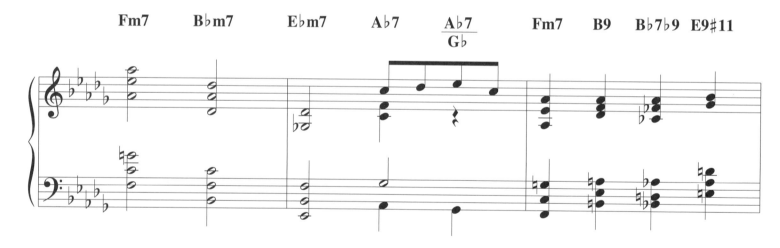

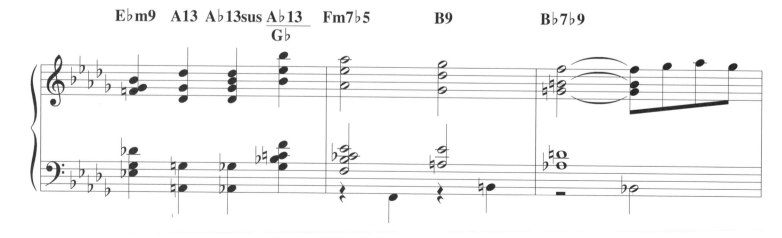

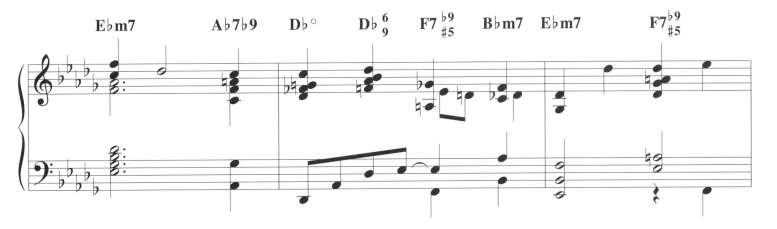

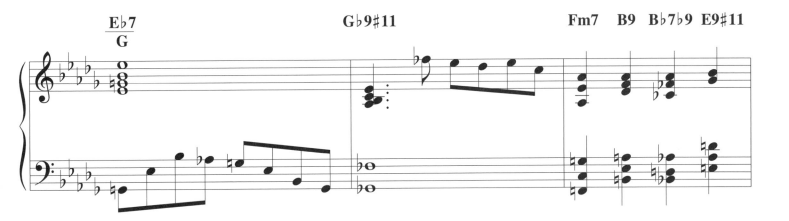

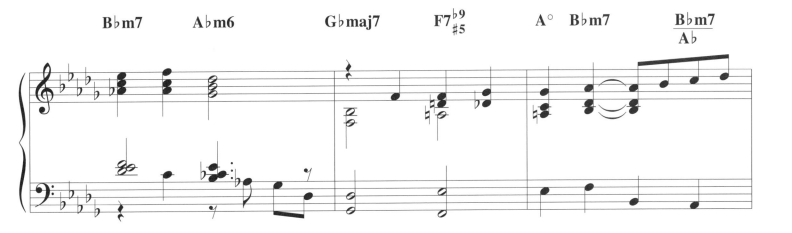

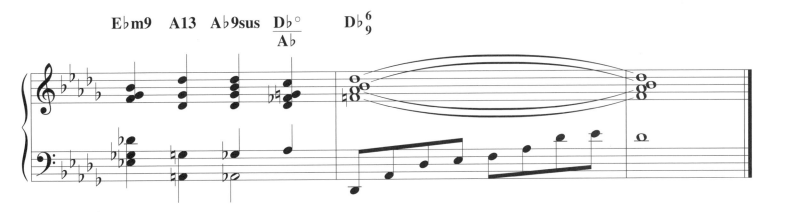

Laurie

Music by BILL EVANS

Medium Ballad

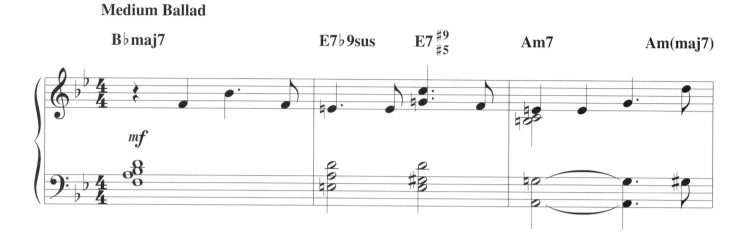

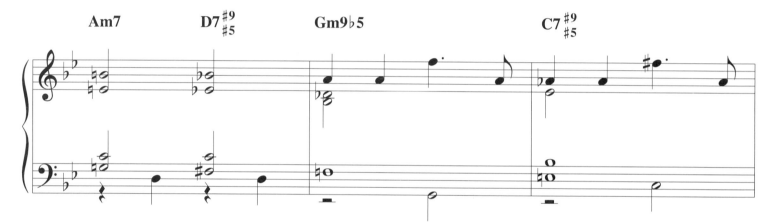

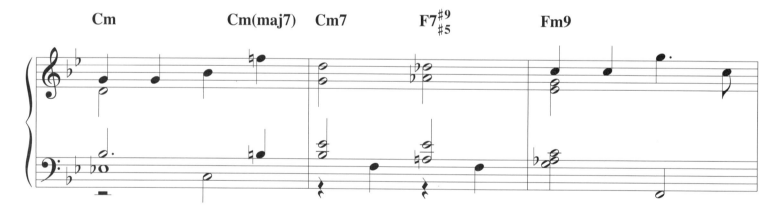

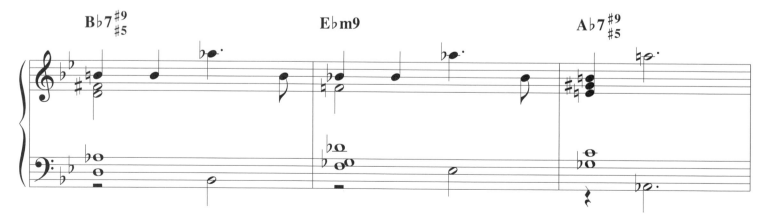

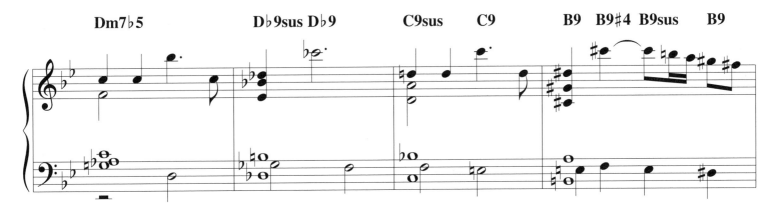

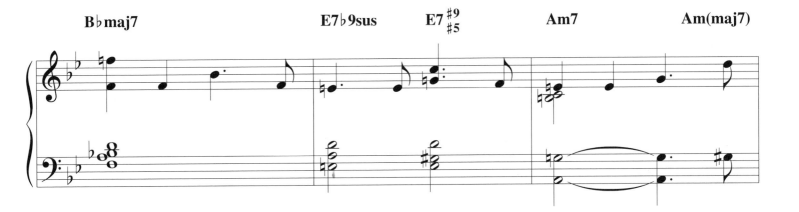

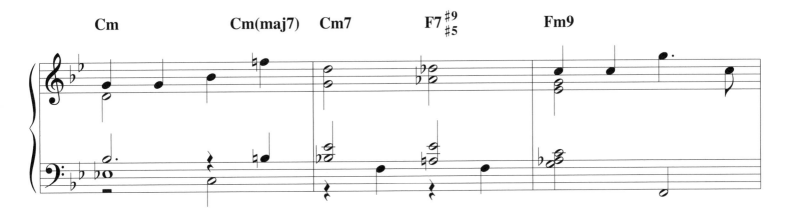

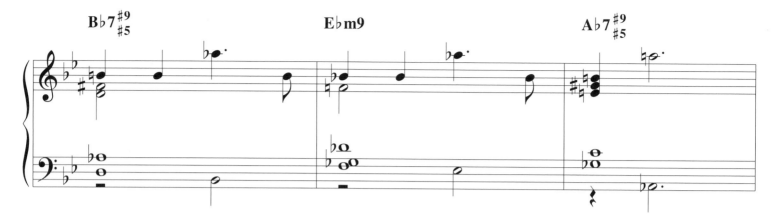

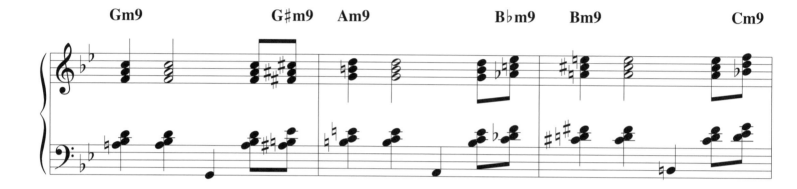

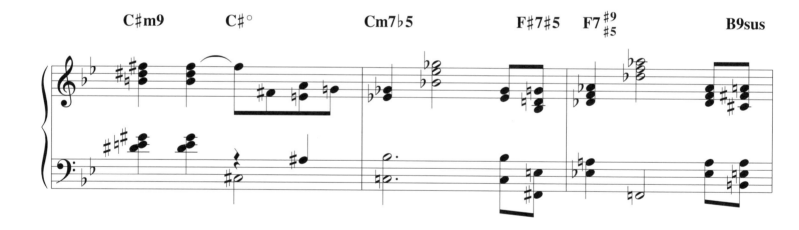

D.C. al Fine

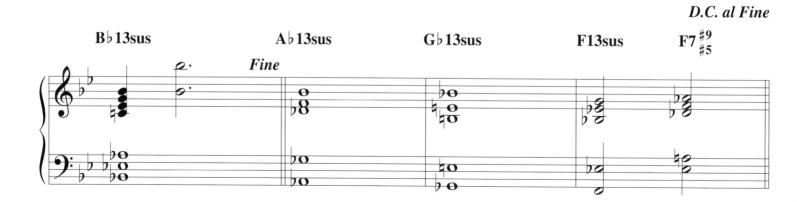

For my son Evan on his 4th birthday, September 13, 1979

Letter to Evan

Music by BILL EVANS

Medium Ballad

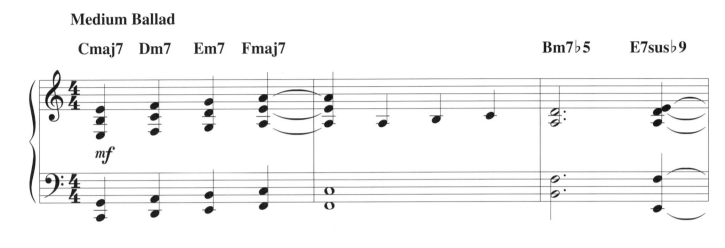

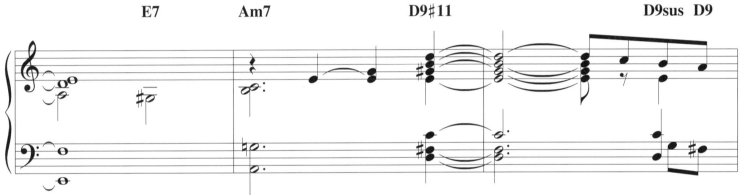

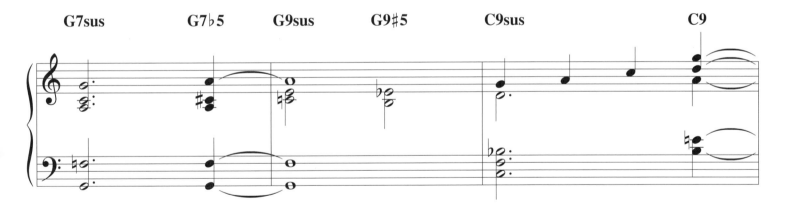

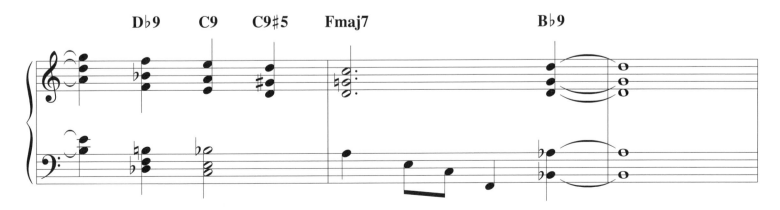

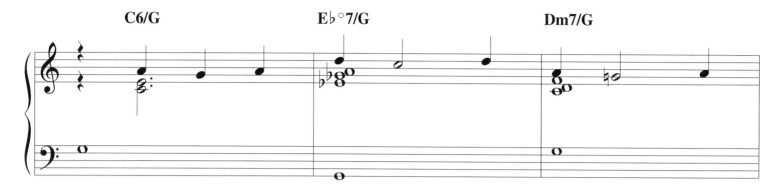

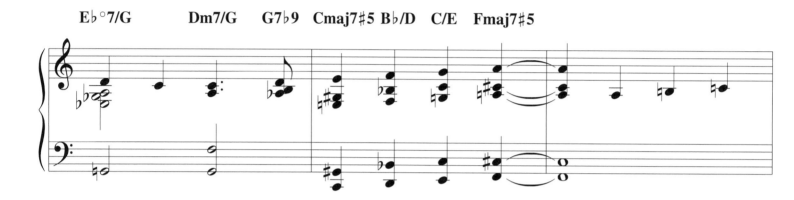

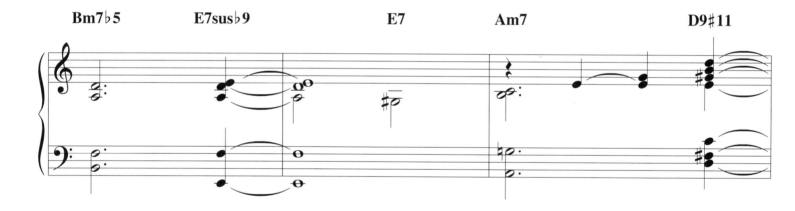

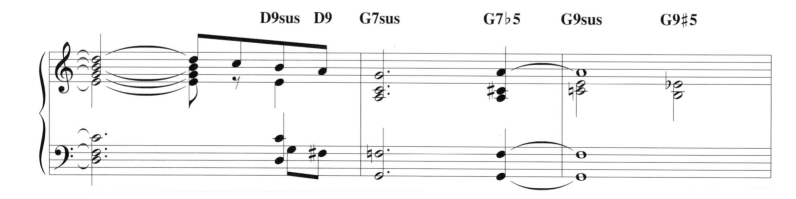

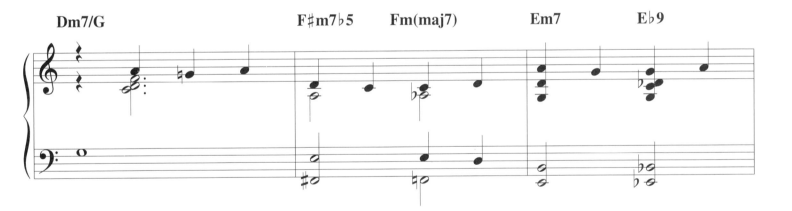

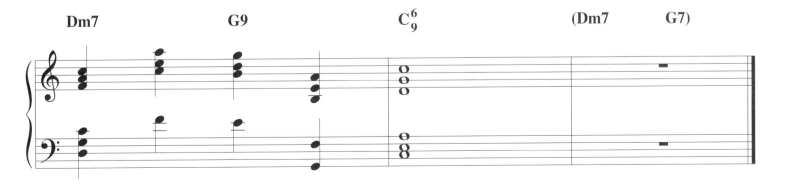

My Bells
(B♭)

Music by BILL EVANS

Medium Ballad

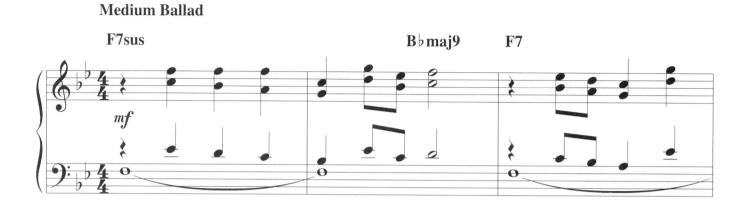

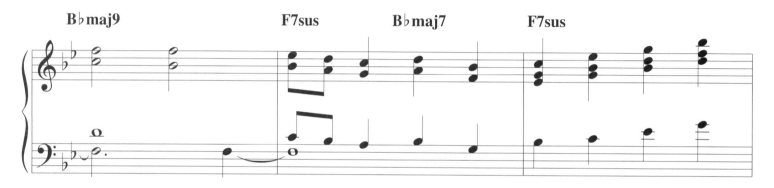

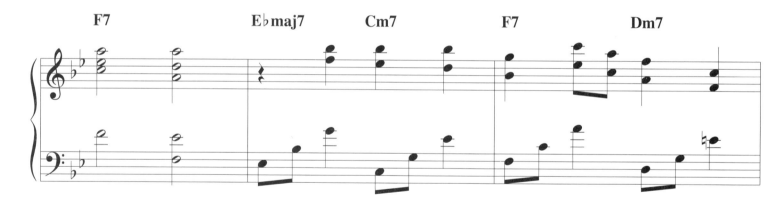

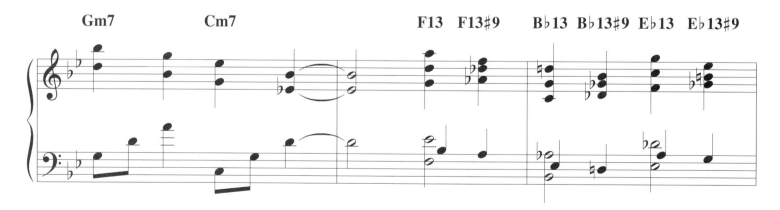

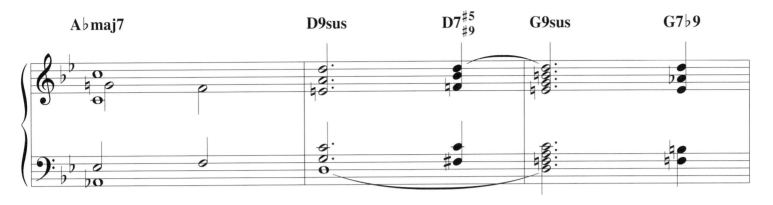

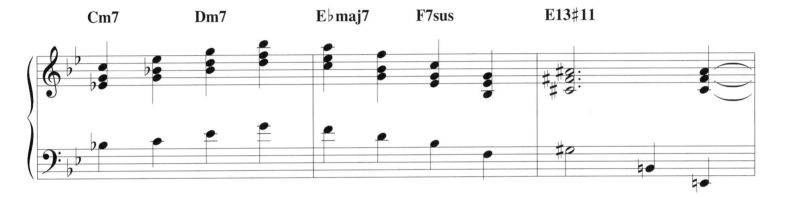

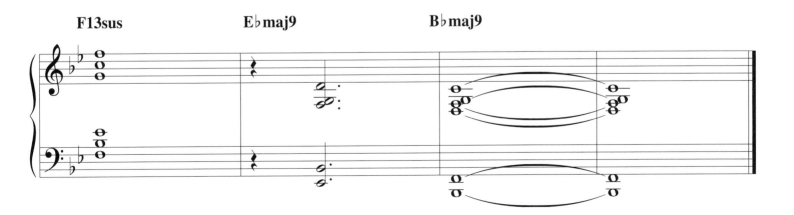

One for Helen

Music by BILL EVANS

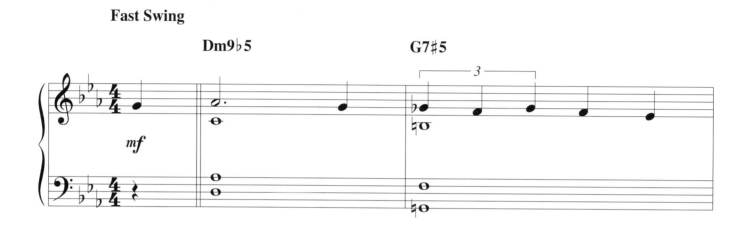

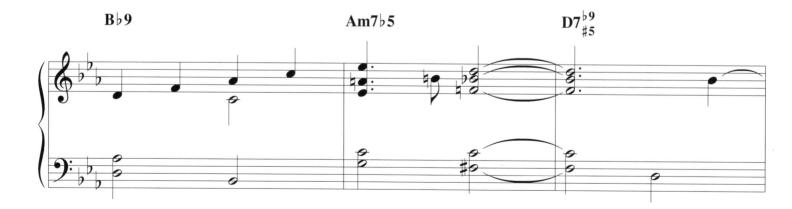

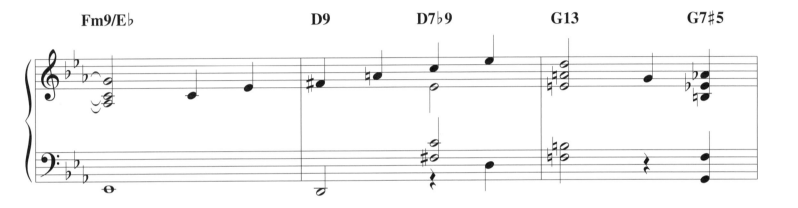

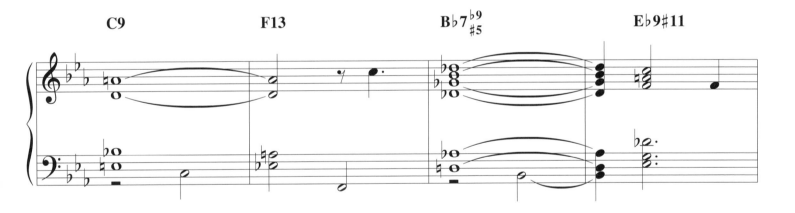

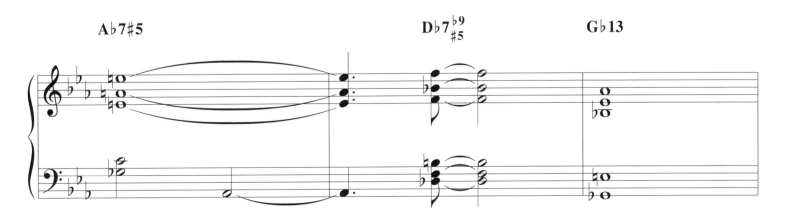

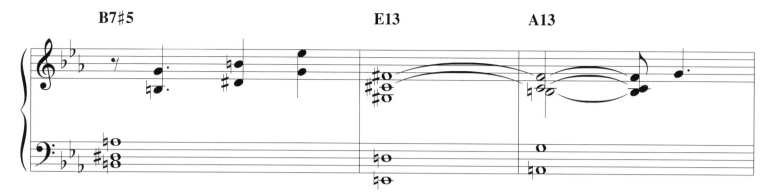

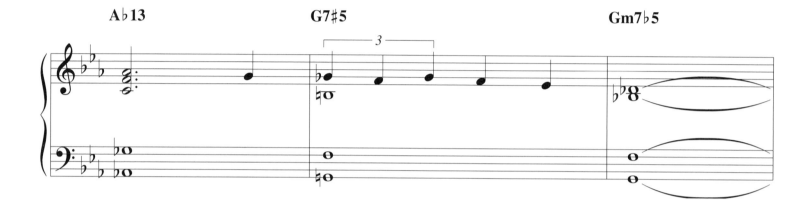

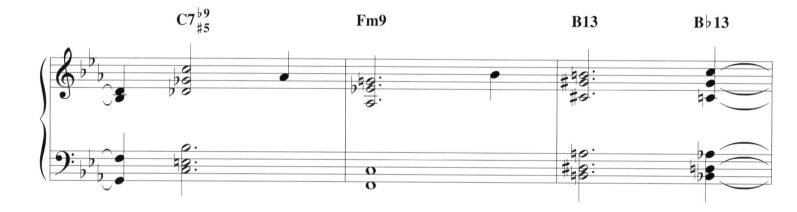

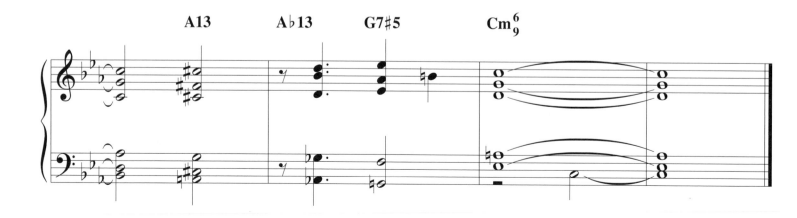

Only Child

Music by BILL EVANS

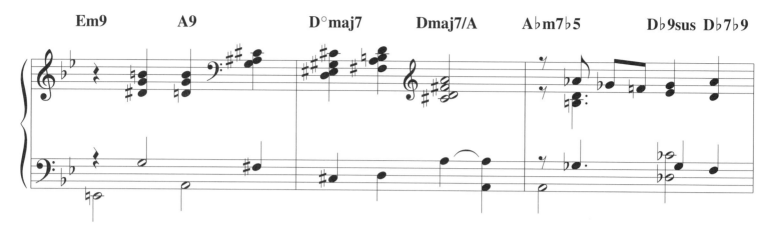

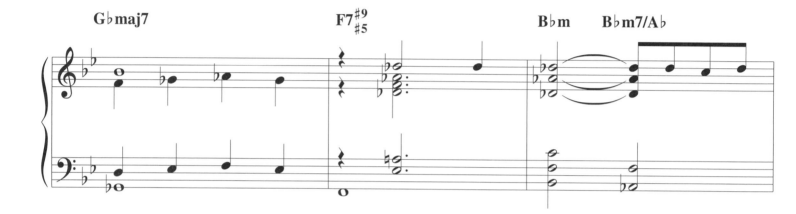

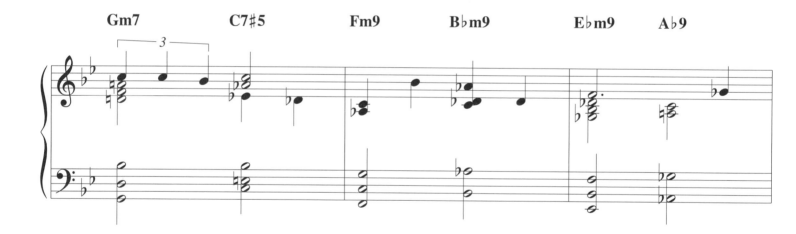

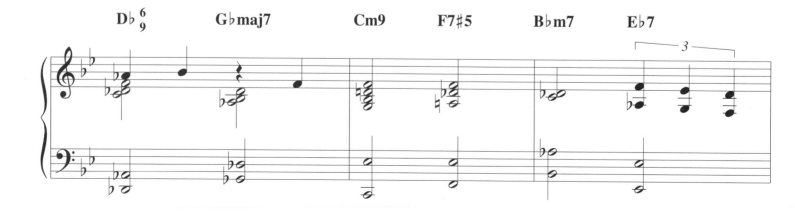

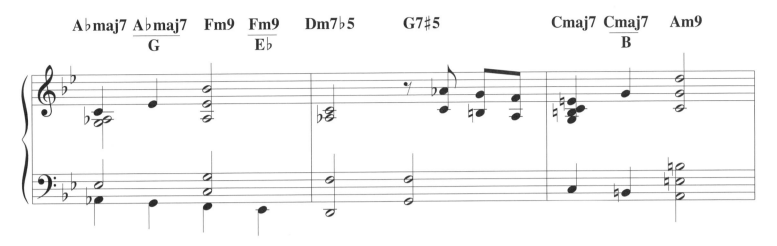

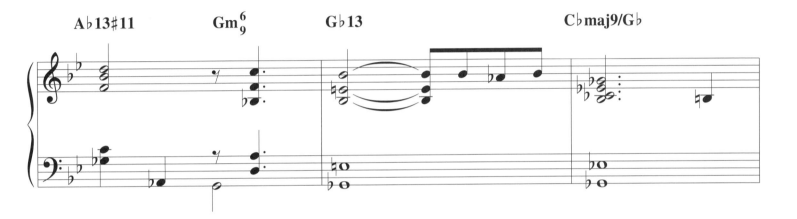

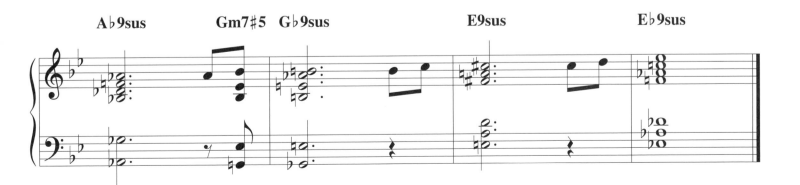

Orbit

Music by BILL EVANS

Medium Swing (in 2)

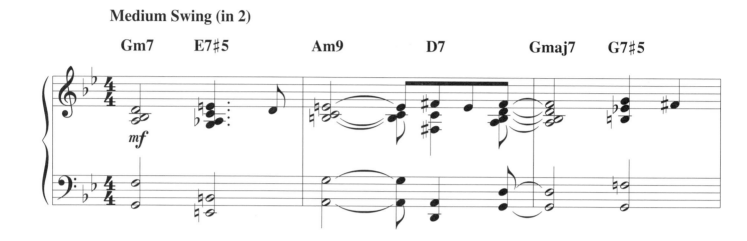

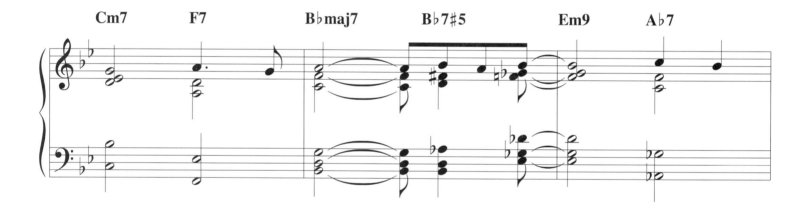

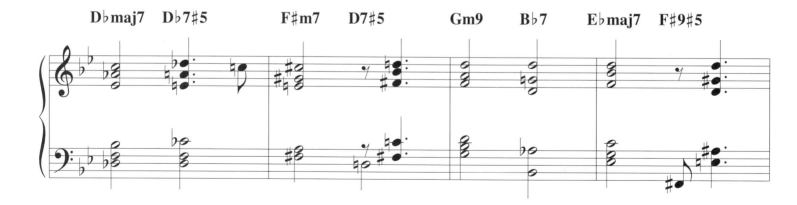

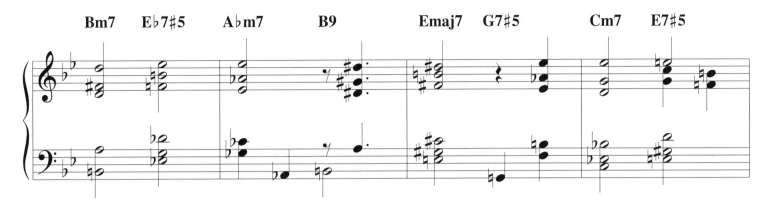

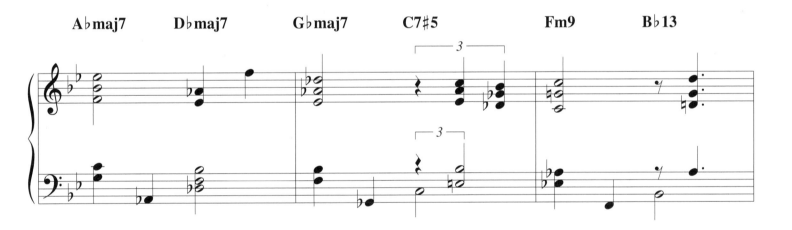

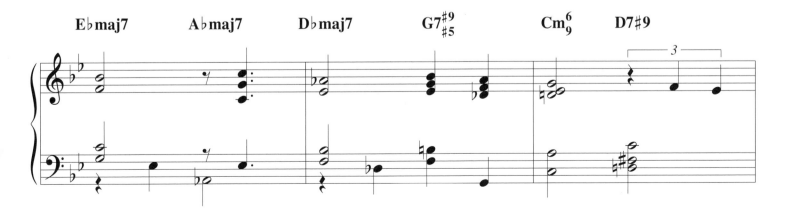

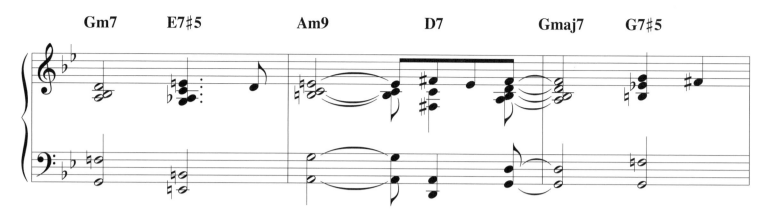

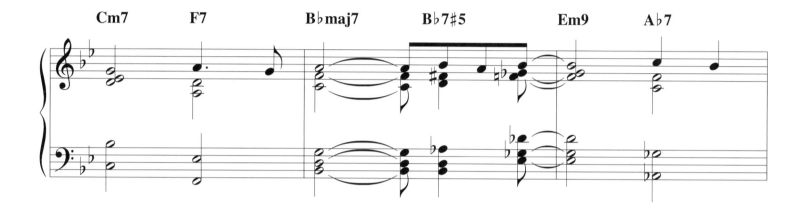

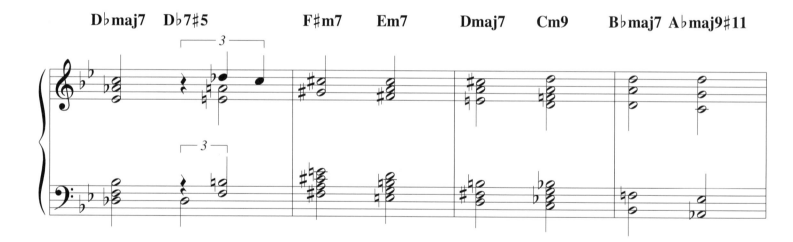

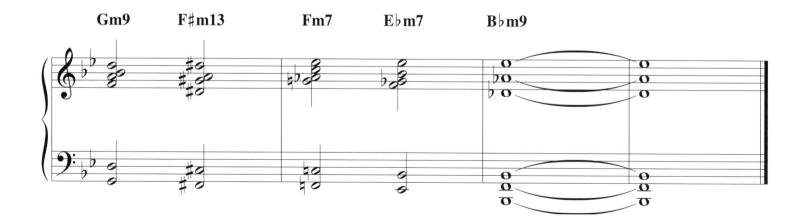

Peace Piece

Music by BILL EVANS

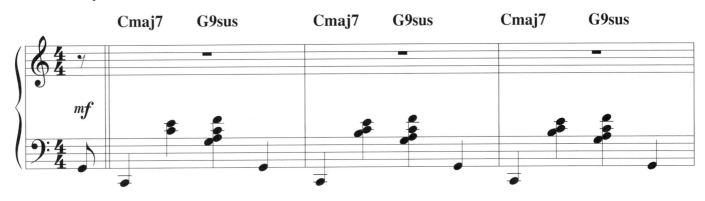

40

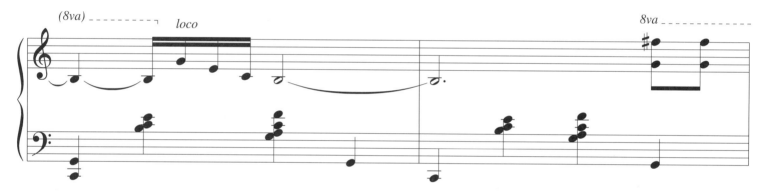

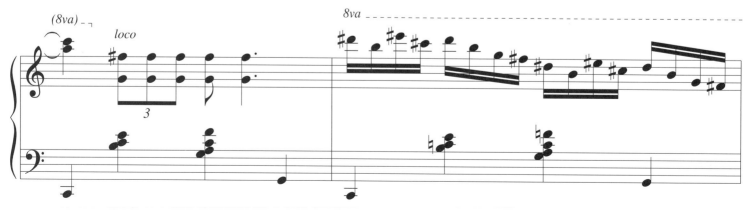

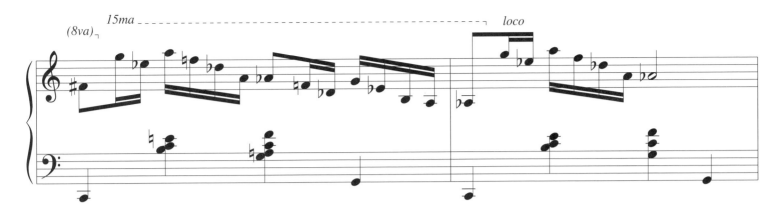

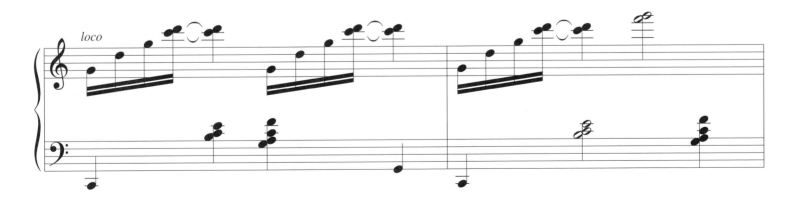

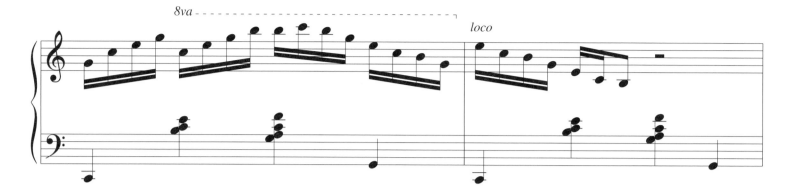

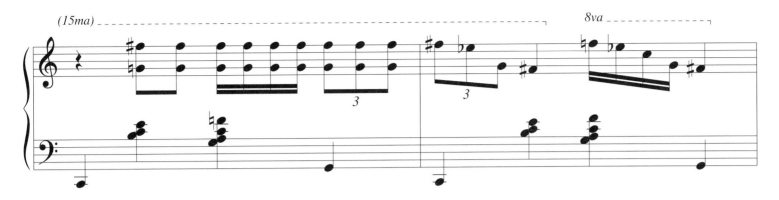

Peri's Scope

Music by BILL EVANS

Medium "Up" Swing

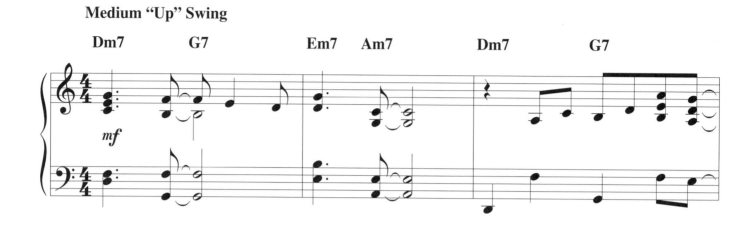

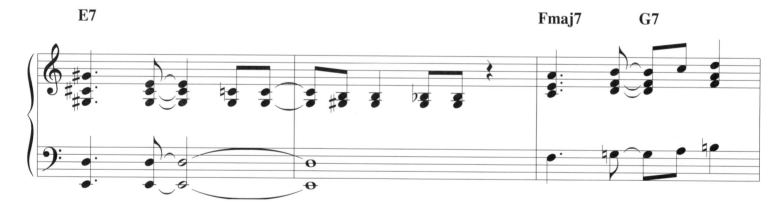

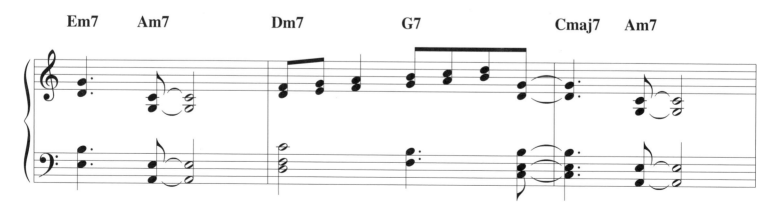

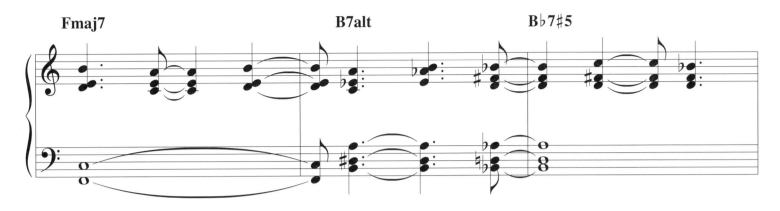

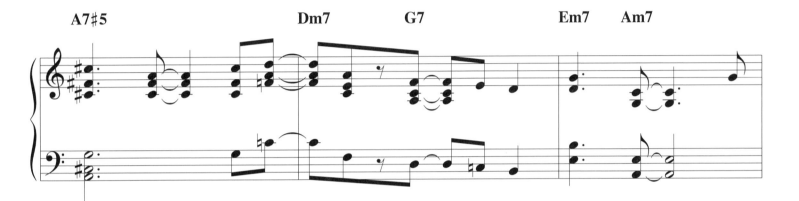

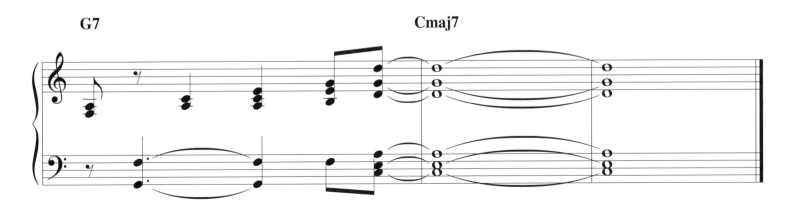

Show-Type Tune
(Tune for a Lyric)

Music by BILL EVANS

Medium Fast Swing ♩ = 108

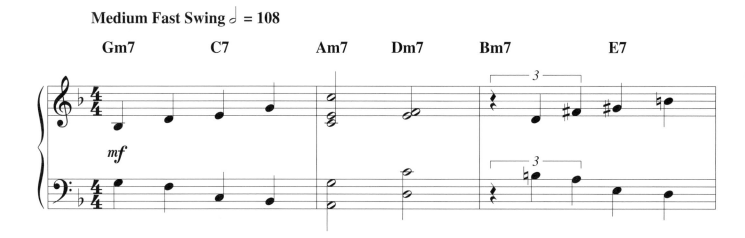

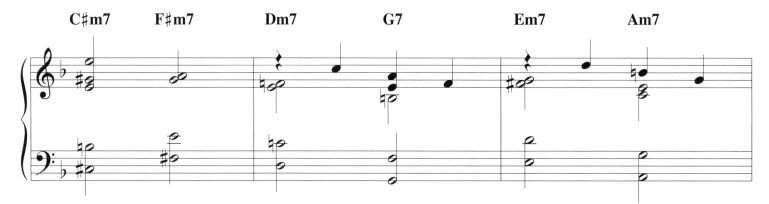

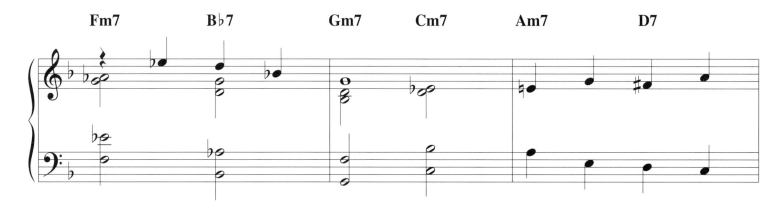

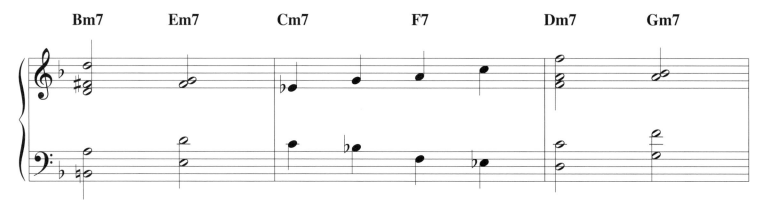

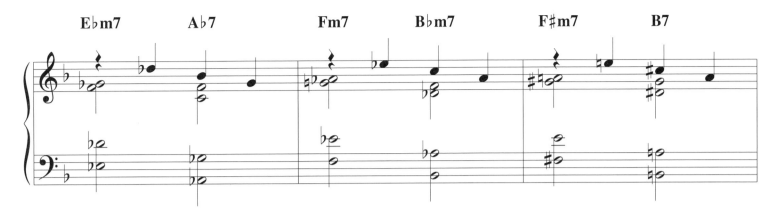

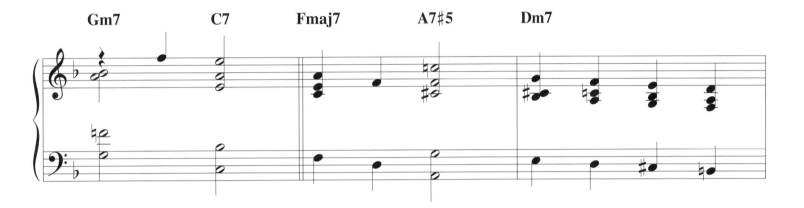

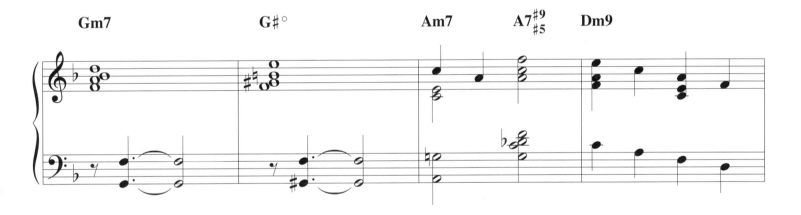

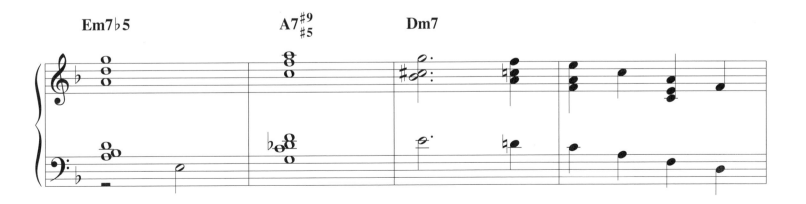

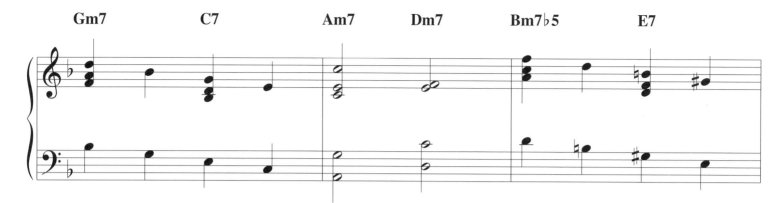

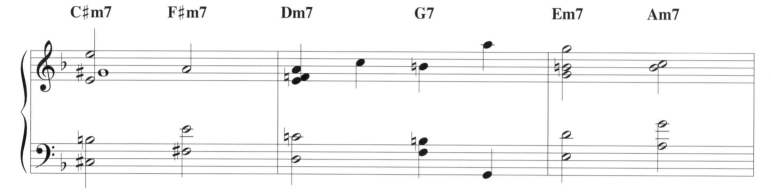

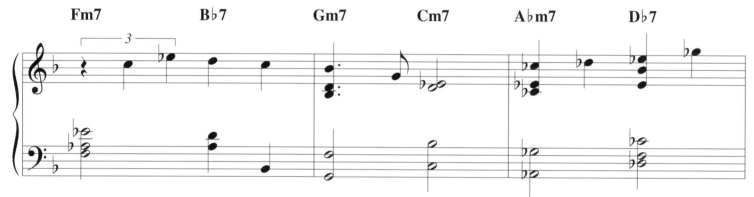

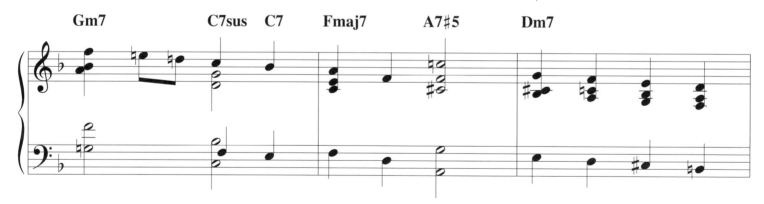

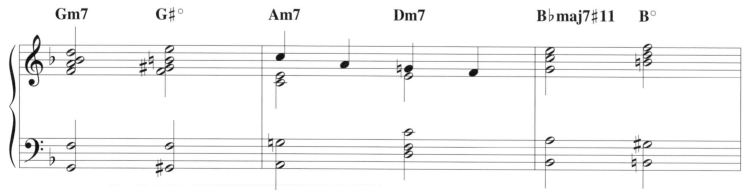

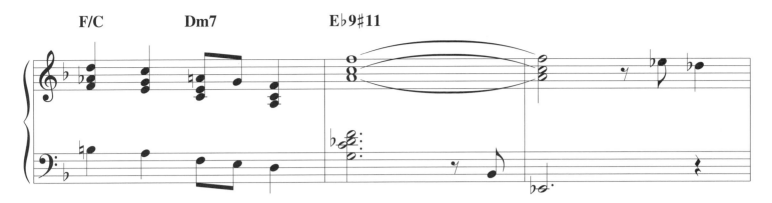

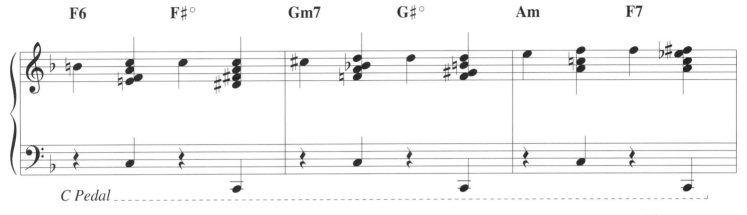

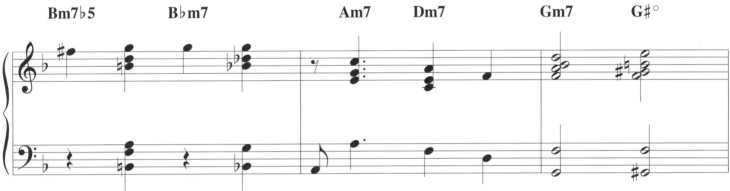

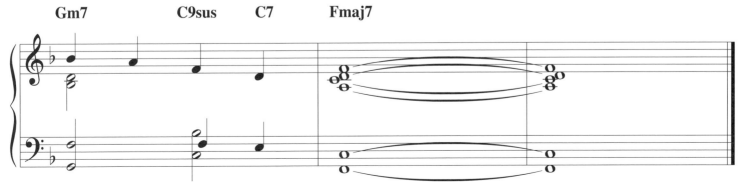

Time Remembered

Music by BILL EVANS

Medium Ballad

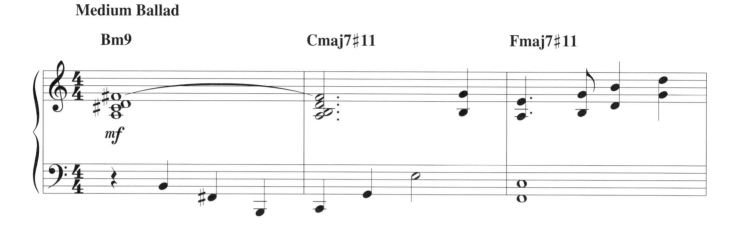

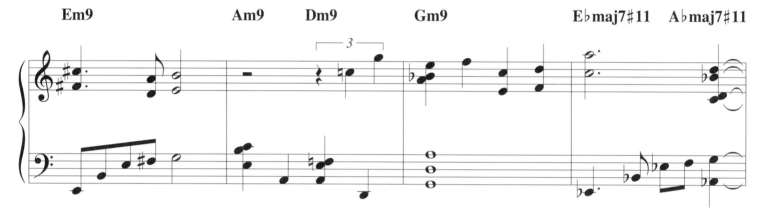

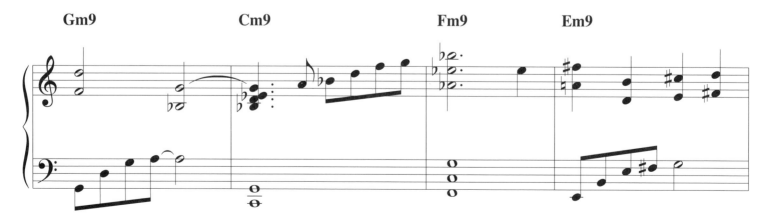

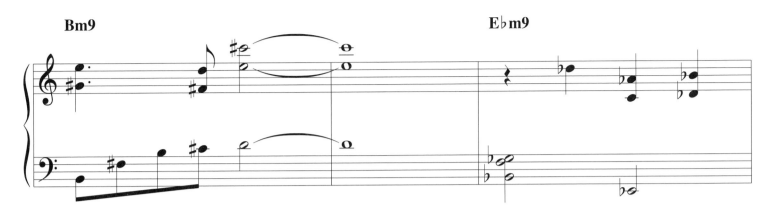

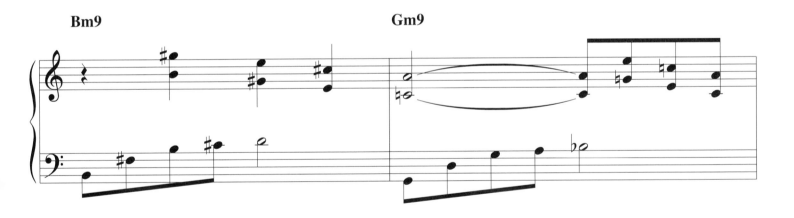

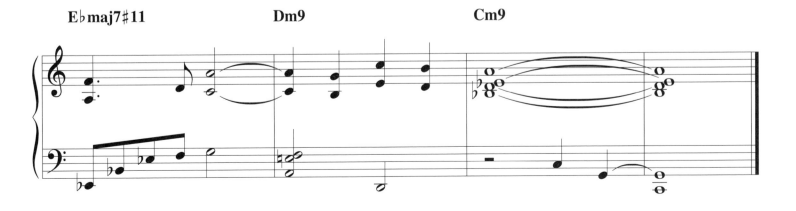

Turn Out the Stars

Lyric by GENE LEES
Music by BILL EVANS

Medium Ballad

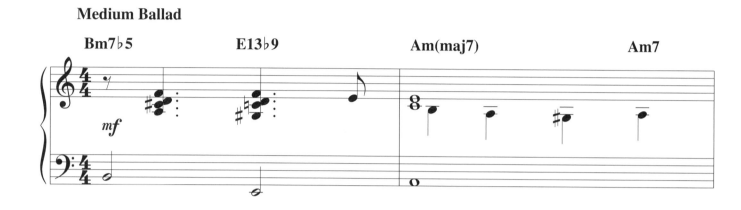

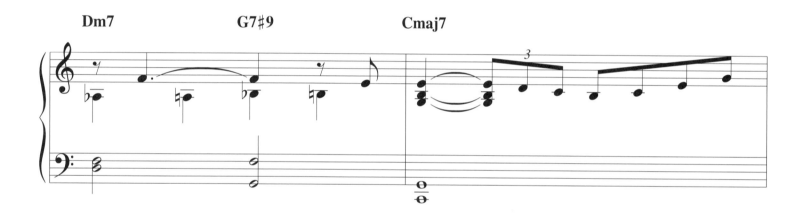

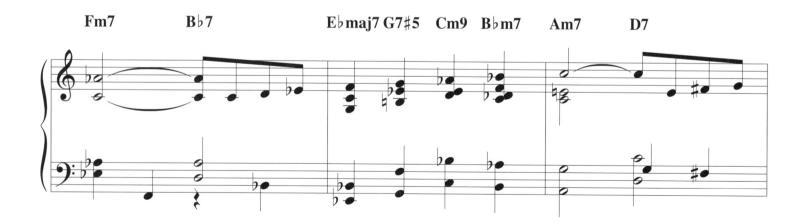

53

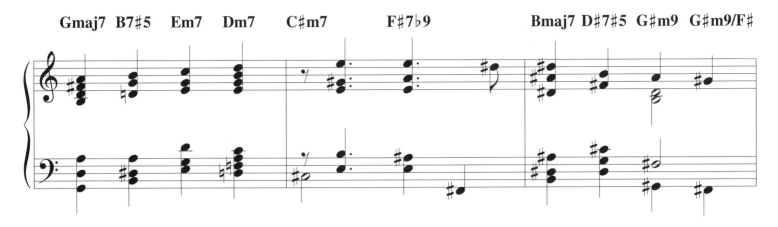

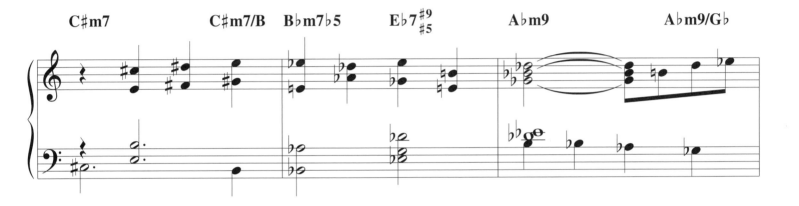

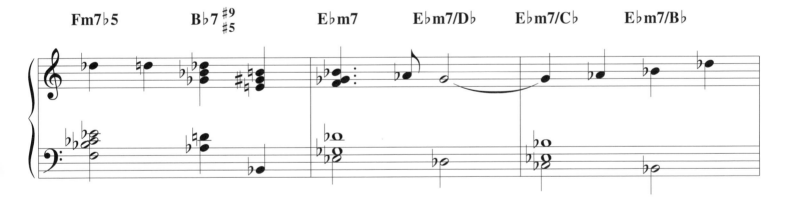

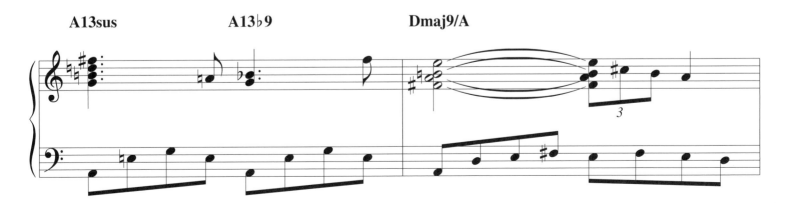

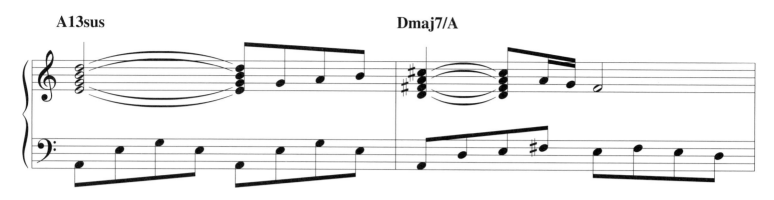

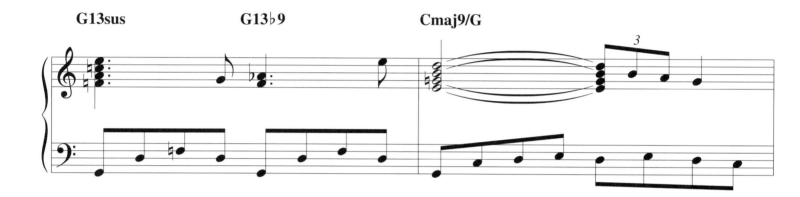

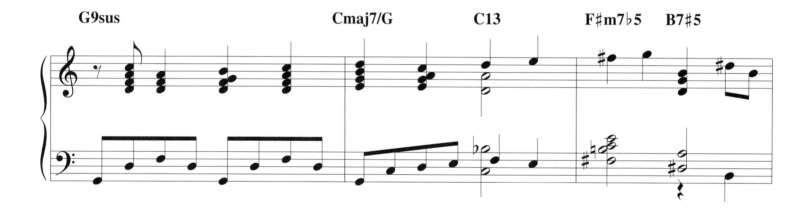

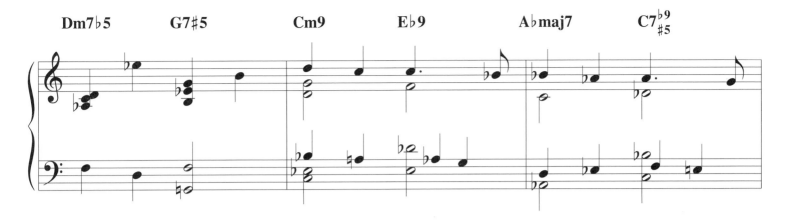

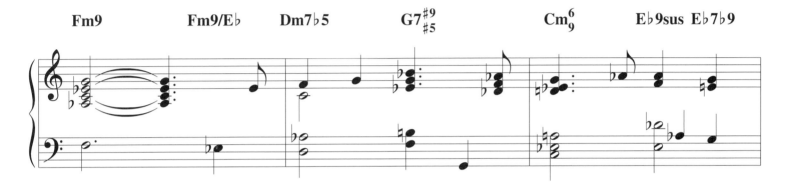

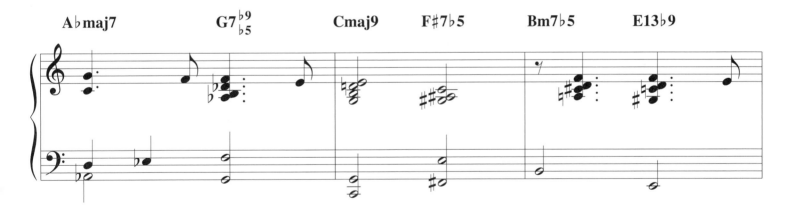

Re: Person I Knew

Music by BILL EVANS

Medium Swing ♩ = 152-168

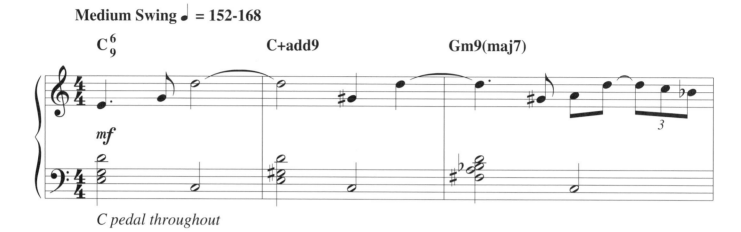

C pedal throughout

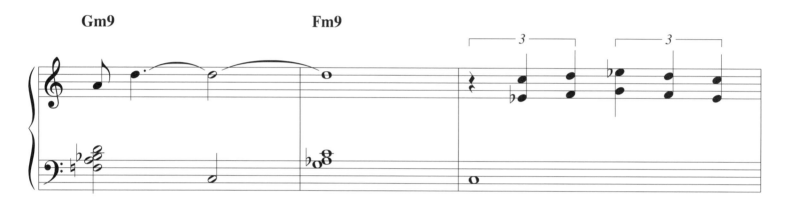

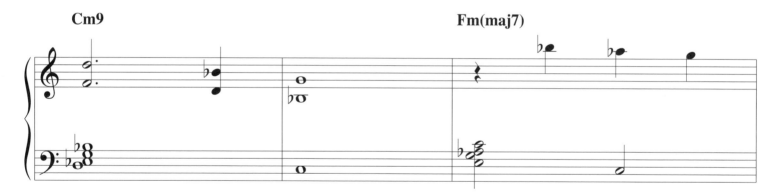

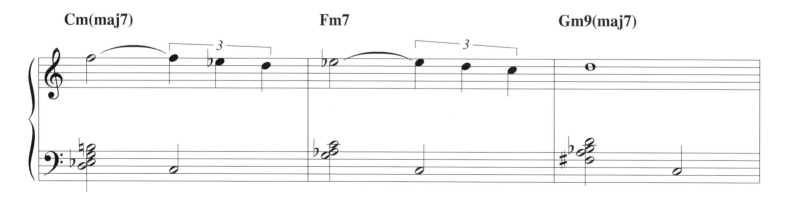

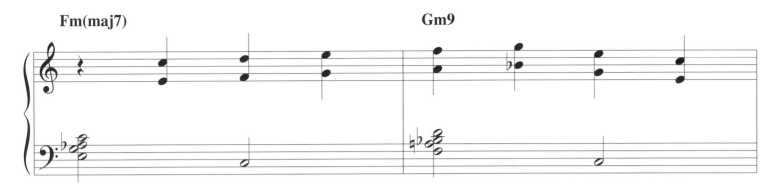

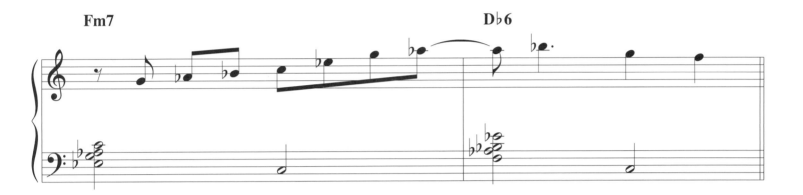

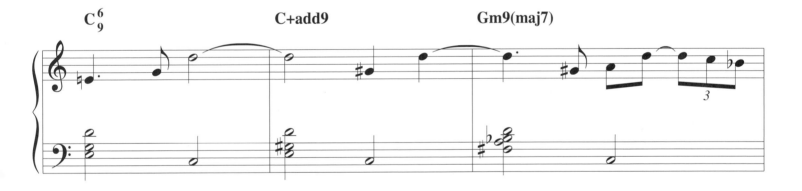

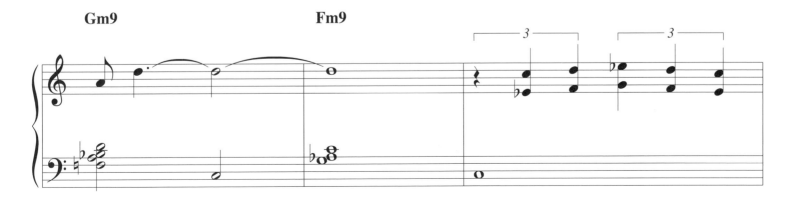

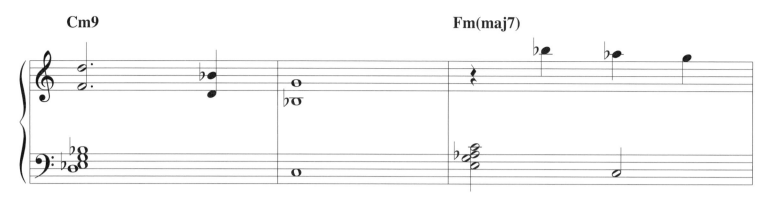

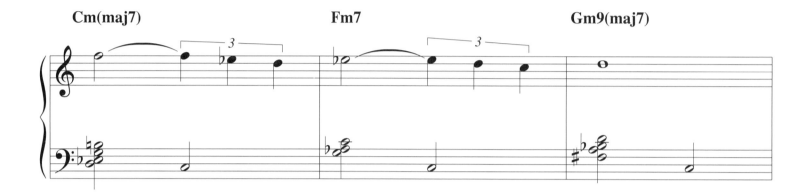

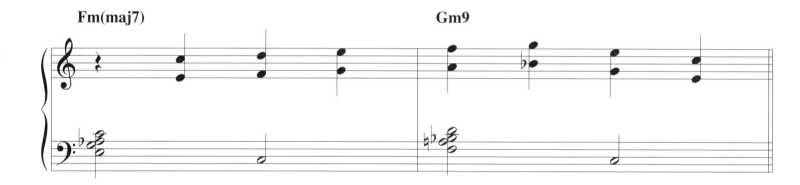

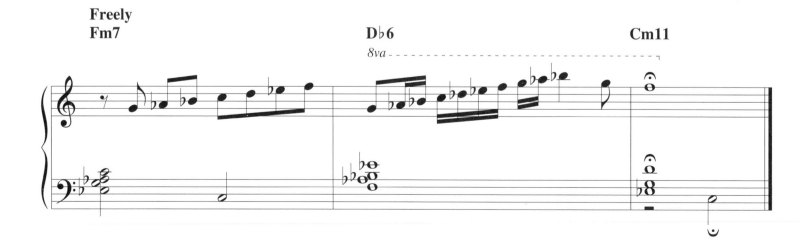

Very Early

Music by BILL EVANS

Medium Jazz Waltz

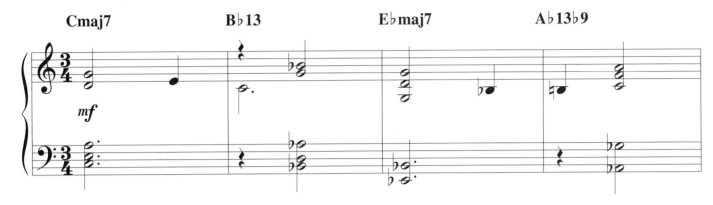

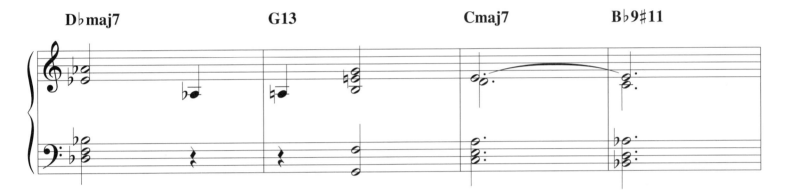

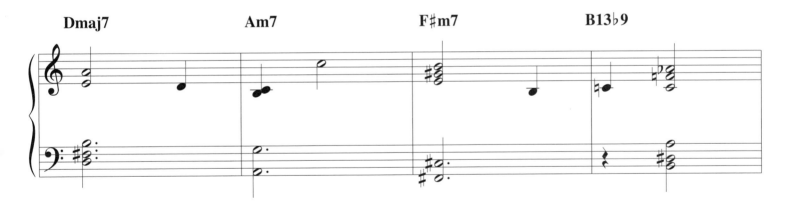

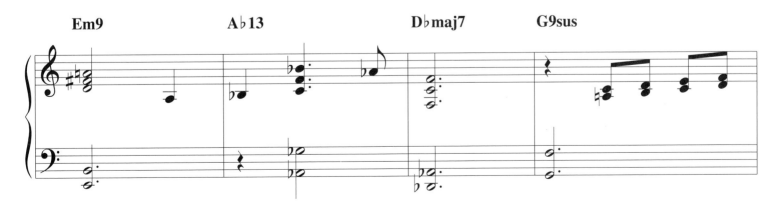

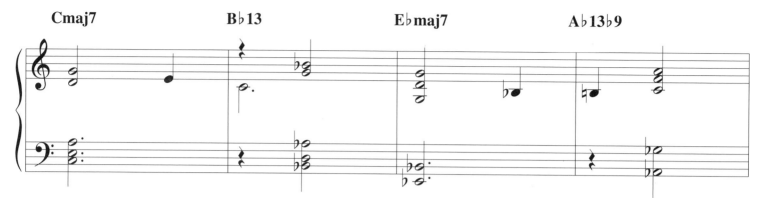

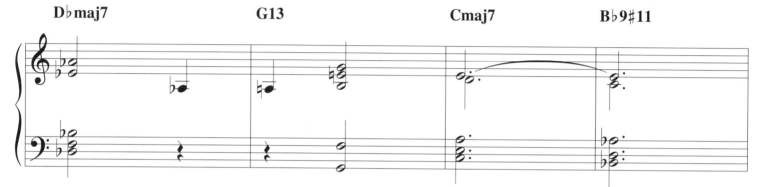

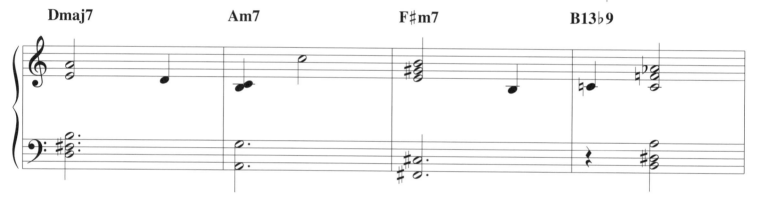

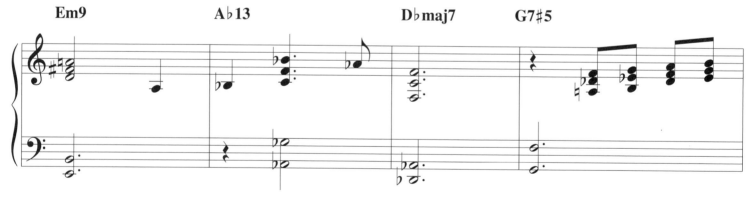

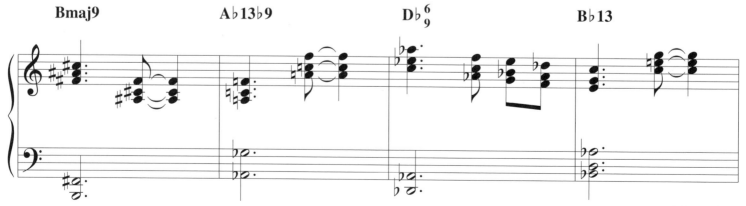

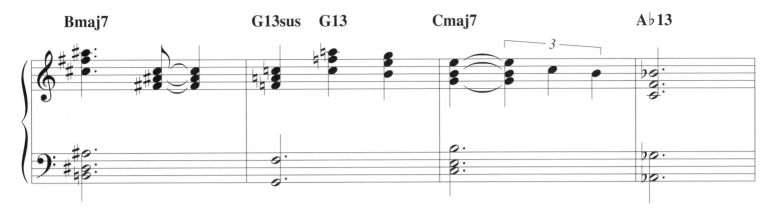

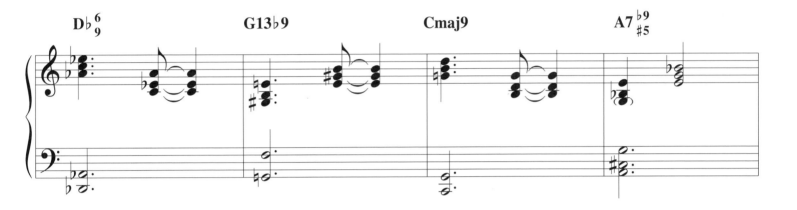

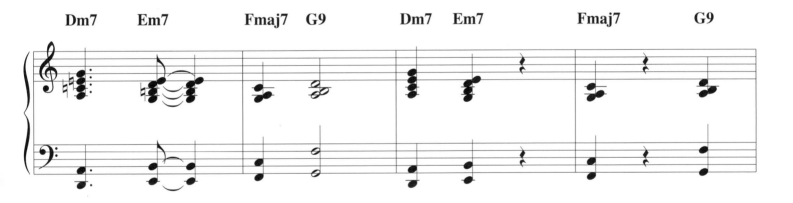

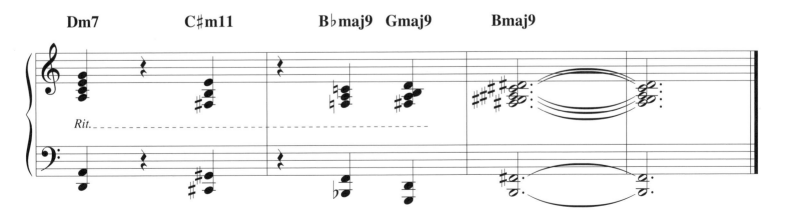

Walkin' Up

Music by BILL EVANS

Fast Swing

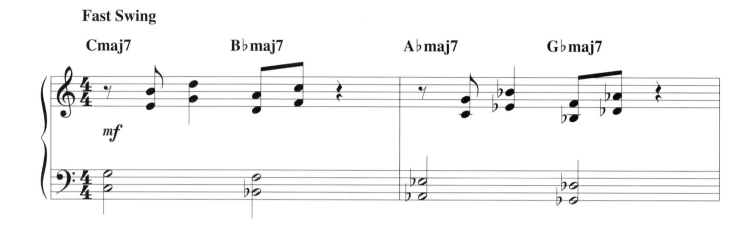

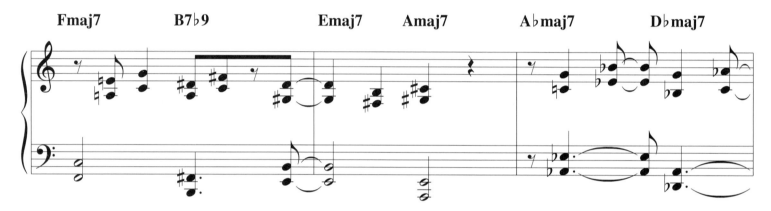

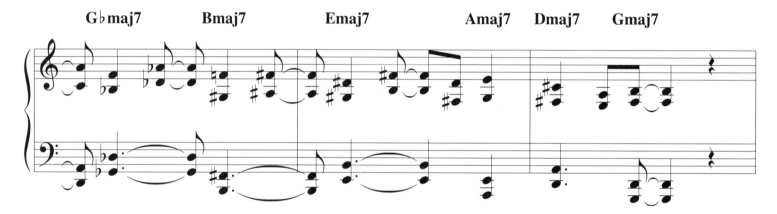

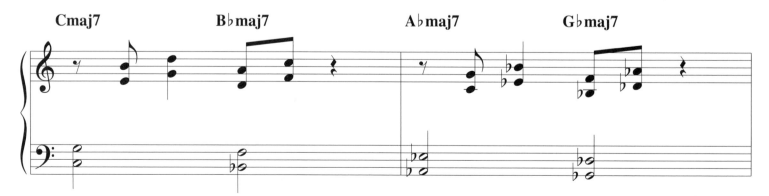

Fmaj7 B7♭9 Emaj7 Amaj7 A♭maj7 D♭maj7

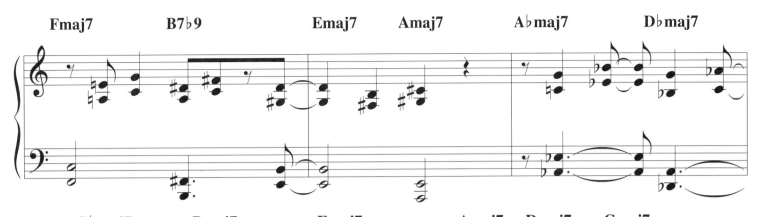

G♭maj7 Bmaj7 Emaj7 Amaj7 Dmaj7 Gmaj7

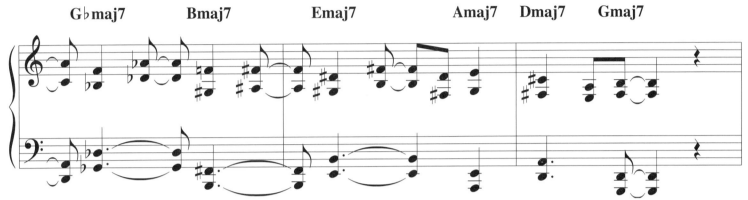

E♭m7/A♭

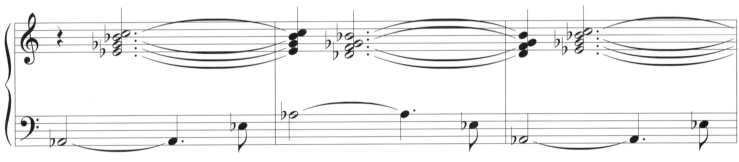

Dm7/G

Cmaj7 B♭maj7

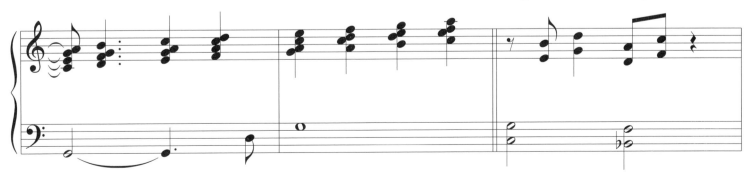

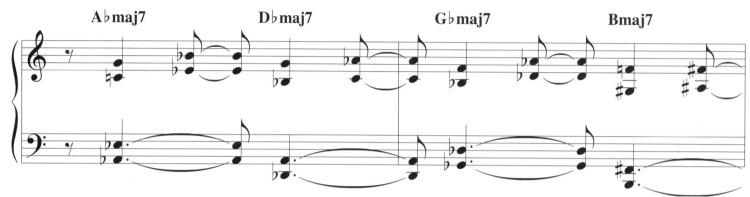

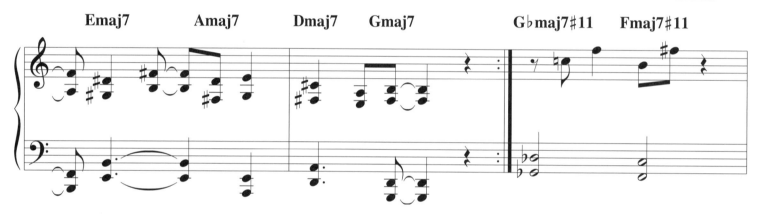

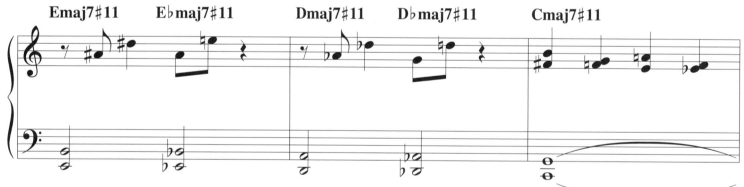

Waltz for Debby

Lyric by GENE LEES
Music by BILL EVANS

Medium Jazz Waltz (in 1)

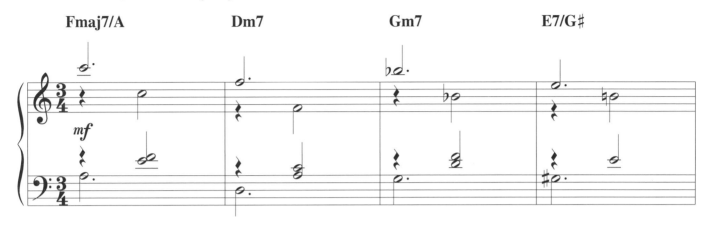

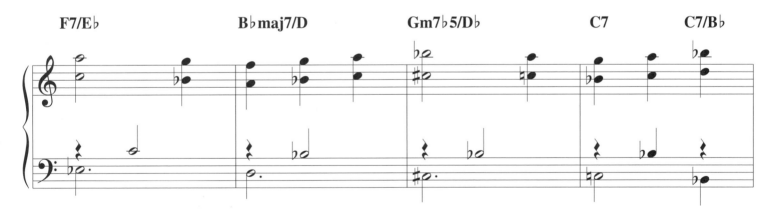

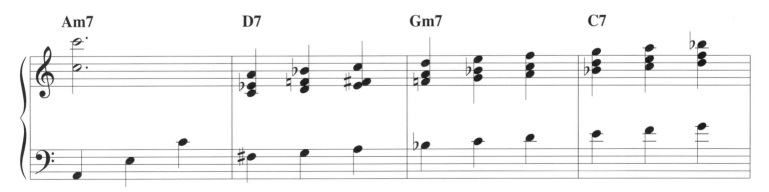

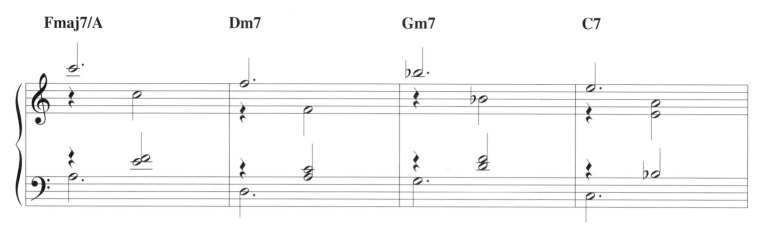

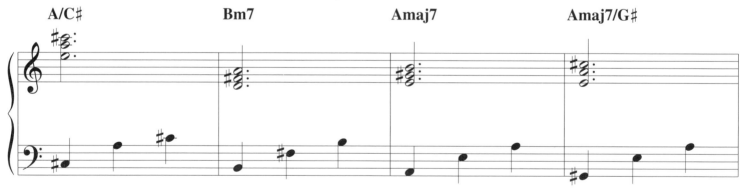

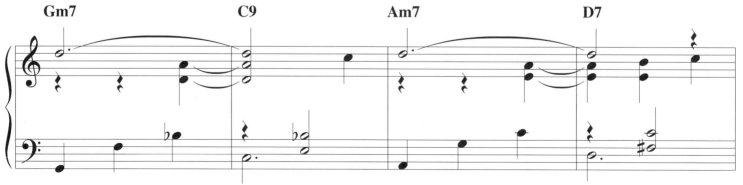

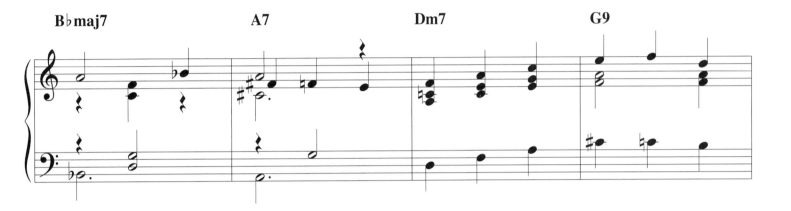

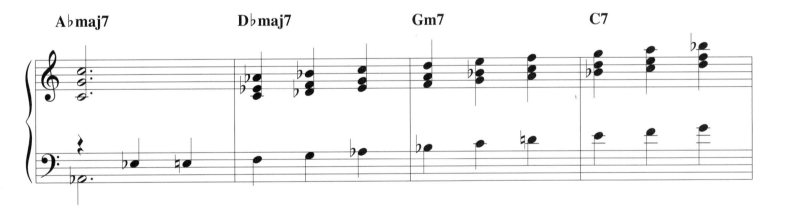

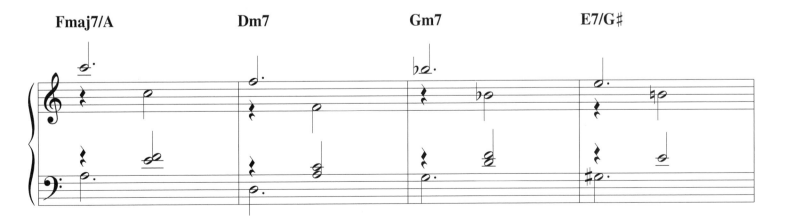

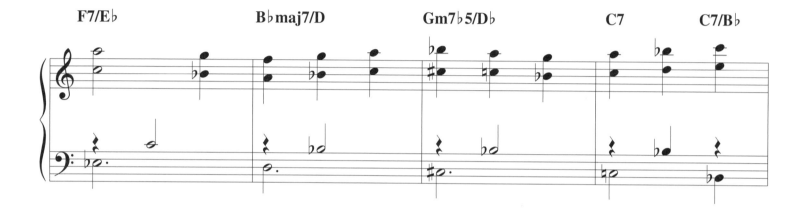

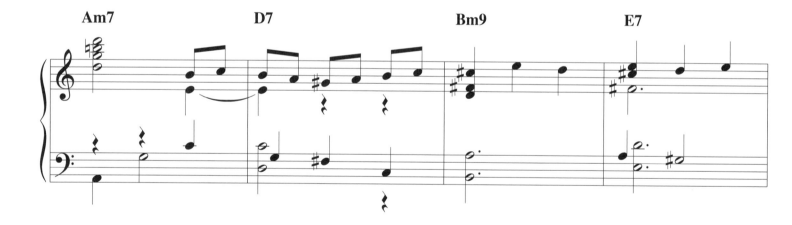

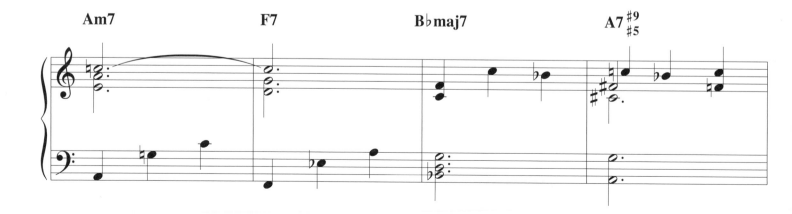

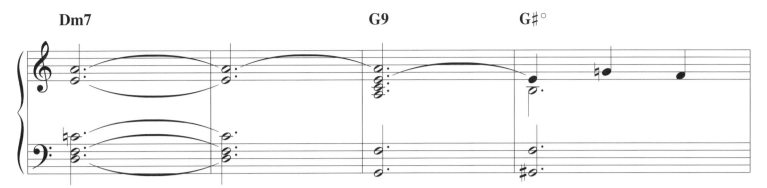

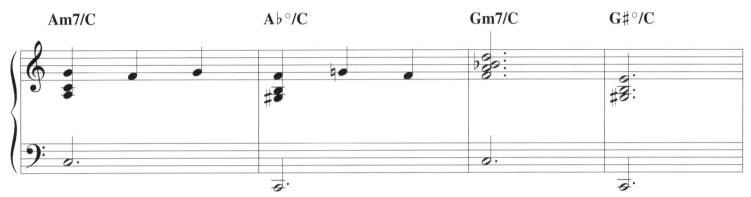

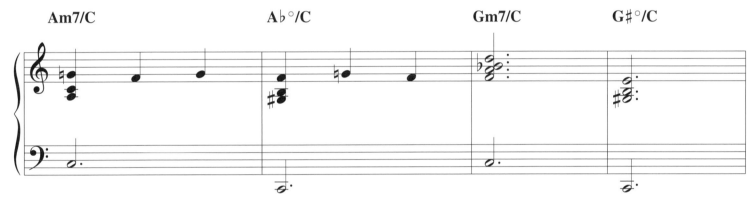

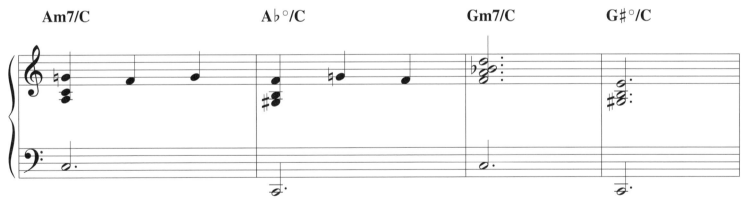

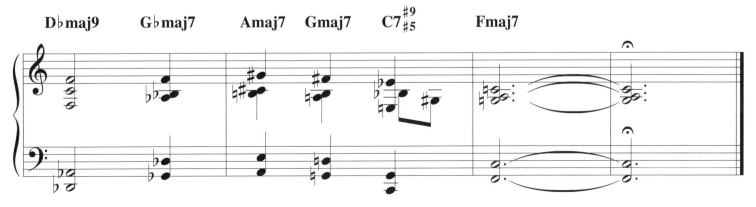

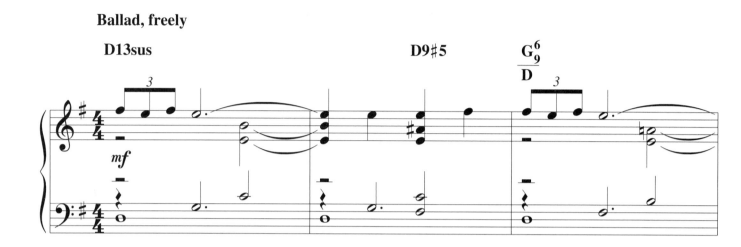

Your Story

Music by BILL EVANS

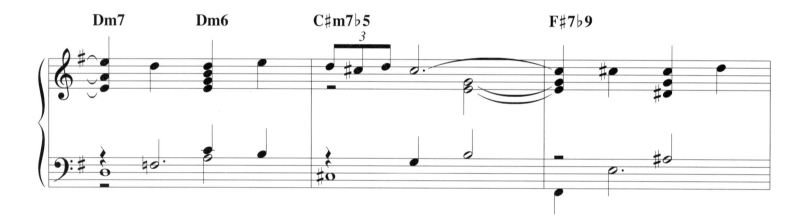

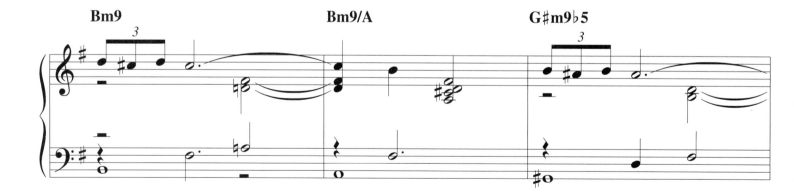

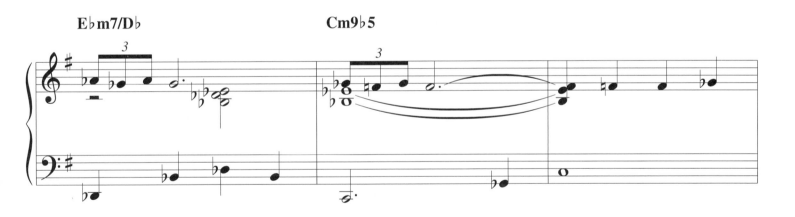

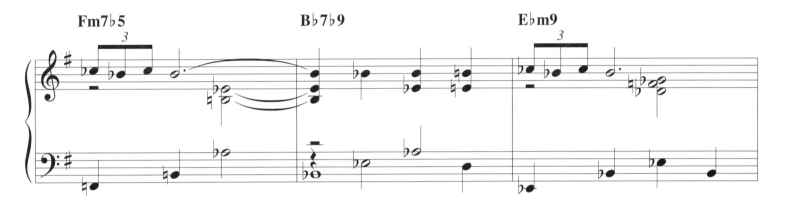

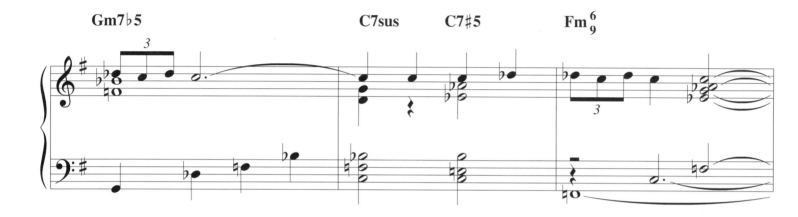

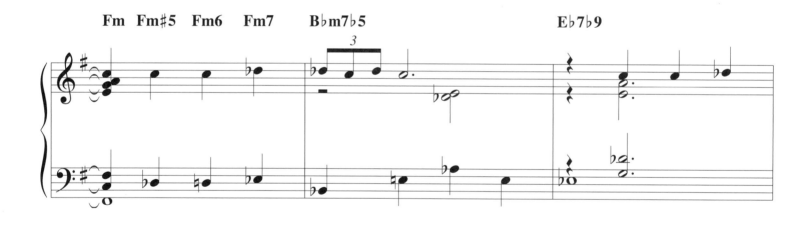

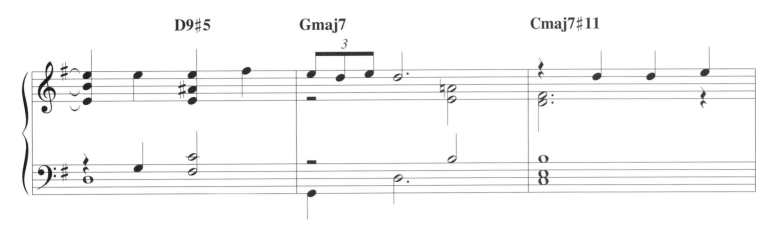

D9#5 Gmaj7 Cmaj7#11

F#m7♭5 B7♭9 Em7

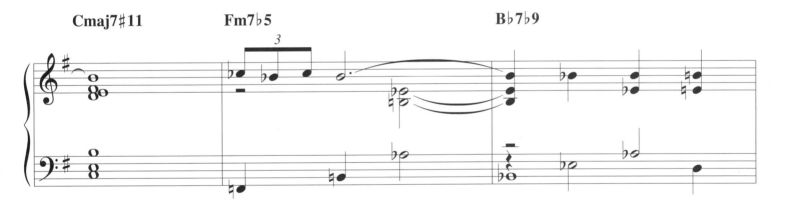

Cmaj7#11 Fm7♭5 B♭7♭9

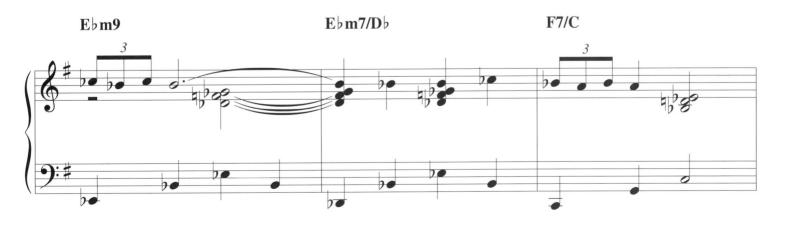

E♭m9 E♭m7/D♭ F7/C

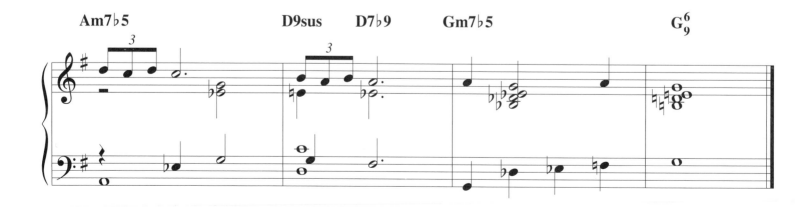

In April
(For Nenette)

Lyric by Roger Schore
Music by Bill Evans

You feel the charm of spring in April,
Something's in the air,
The world's a playground swing in April.
Suddenly the sunshine discloses
Soon there'll be roses,
Your heart proposes twice a day.
Imagine!

Love blossoms all around in April,
Not a single care,
Your lonely heart has found a home today,
And in the space of a minute,
You're swept up in it,
With luck you'll win it, your spring bouquet.
That happy ending,
A love in April that will stay.

Your life has just begun in April,
Joy is everywhere,
Due to that special one in April.
He can make a cottage a tower,
A bud a flower,
An April shower a surprise.
Imagine!

Love is the only game in April,
Nothing can compare
When Cupid plans to aim his lethal dart.
Then you'll take leave of your senses,
Drop all defenses,
As he commences to do his part.
When you start falling
And April steals away your heart.

Very Early

Lyric by Carol Hall
Music by Bill Evans

Very early love came quickly when I first saw you.
You were all I ever wanted.
Strange how early I knew!

Very early I came running like an eager child.
Love was all I ever asked for.
Love came wondrous and wild!

Now the early rain beats on my window,
Sweet the sound rain can make.
Nice to lie here, softly sigh here,
You and I here, waiting for the very early sun to wake.

Laurie
(The Dream)

Lyric by Bob Dorough
Music by Bill Evans

Deep in a dream
I stir and speak the name of her
When I call Laurie.
Is she real or is she just a name I dreamed of, Laurie?

Sweet indecision,
Sweet lovely vision.
See her come smiling!
Charming!
Beguiling!

Then I tumble down.
Out on the street
I hear the sound of traffic
While I look for Laurie.
Searching every face
But still no trace is there of Laurie.

Sweet inspiration,
In sweet desperation
I sleep once again
But to dream
For it seems that Laurie
Only loves me when I'm dreaming.

For my son Evan on his 4th birthday, September 13, 1979

Letter to Evan

Words and Music by Bill Evans

Is there a place that is all willing?
Is there a heart that is all beauty?
Is there a love that's every answer?
I write this letter just once, my son,
There is no more.

Your mind is the place that all is willing.
You have the heart that is all beauty.
You are the love that's every answer.
Just listen: mmm,
There is but this one music,
Evan, you will need no other star.

My Bells

Lyric by Gene Lees
Music by Bill Evans

On Sundays when I was small,
I'd awake and lie there
In the music of bells that filled the morning.

I'd hear my bells ringing out,
Singing out,
Flinging out to the air
Carefree.
A promise of the silver days before me.

But then the years hurried by
And my bells fell silent,
And I asked how the skies could lose their brightness.

Somehow, I had lost my way,
Searching here,
Searching there, everywhere,
Careworn.
Until the day you turned around and found me.

Suddenly all my bells are once more singing.
Listen now,
And I'm sure you'll hear them ring for you.

Only Child

Lyric by Roger Schore
Music by Bill Evans

My one and only child
Dear as a child can be,
You'll never know how much you mean to me.
One day you're climbing trees
And chasing dragonflies,
Next day, well look who's grown
Right before my eyes.

Time moves on
And in the blink of an eye,
You're here and gone,
The years go racing by.
One day you'll fall in love
Like no one's ever known.
Some day, my only child,
You'll love a child of your own.

Time Remembered

Lyric by Paul Lewis
Music by Bill Evans

Time remembered.
Remember spring as you walk past a frozen lake in winter.
Listen, the music calls you.
Let it take you away to glist'ning shores where dolphins play,
Back to your quiet mind where colors change in time.
Rememberered lines
Lead to the love inside remembered time.

You feel the time inside you.
You're looking down at your hands and the room fills up with angels.
Take them, show them the way
To magnificent skies and em'rald hills where giants play.
And though they're going to cheer,
They really want to hear
Those quiet lines
That lead them back inside remembered time.

Time remembered.
Remember spring as you sleep through the iron days of winter.
How then could we repay you?
In your moment on earth, you taught us to believe in spring.
And when your heart went still,
What did you find there, Bill?
Play just one line.
Show us what lies beyond remembered time.

Turn Out the Stars

Lyric by Gene Lees
Music by Bill Evans

Turn out the stars, turn out the stars.
Let eternal darkness hide me if I can't have you beside me.
Put out their fires.
Their endless splendor only reminds me of your tenderness.

Stop the ocean's roar.
Don't let the rivers run.
Let me hear no more the wondrous music of a skylark in the sun.
Let it be done.
Turn out the stars, turn out the stars, shut off their light.
Stop every comet in its magic, lonely flight.
Let there be night.
Turn out the stars.

Dawn Preludes

(Time Remembered)

Lyric by Karen Gallinger
Music by Bill Evans

Dawn, I feel the sun begin to rise;
Hearing you sigh as you sleep here in my arms,
Feeling your heartbeat, the flutter of a bird.
It sings to me of our new love.
I watch you sleeping here and gently touch your face;
I kiss your lips and draw you near:
A prelude to our loving.

Dawn, the sun proclaims the coming day;
A secret smile as I watch you,
Shadows and daylight vying to touch your velvet skin.
I gently reach to waken you;
Your golden flesh is warm, your sleepy eyes meet mine;
We laugh out loud and greet the day:
A prelude to our living.

Dawn, my heart envies the light,
Its touch daring not to reach my own hand;
My fear of waking you bearing witness to the distance sadly now between us.
I memorize your face, the last dawn we will share,
This time will be remembered as
A prelude to your leaving.

Waltz for Debby

Lyric by Gene Lees
Music by Bill Evans

In her own sweet world,
    populated by dolls and clowns and a prince and a big purple bear,
Lives my favorite girl,
    unaware of the worried frowns that we weary grownups all wear.

In the sun, she dances to silent music,
    songs that are spun of gold somewhere in her own little head.

One day all too soon,
    she'll grow up and she'll leave her dolls and her prince and her silly old bear.
When she goes they will cry,
    as they whisper goodbye.
They will miss her, I fear,
    but then so will I.

BILL EVANS COLLECTIONS

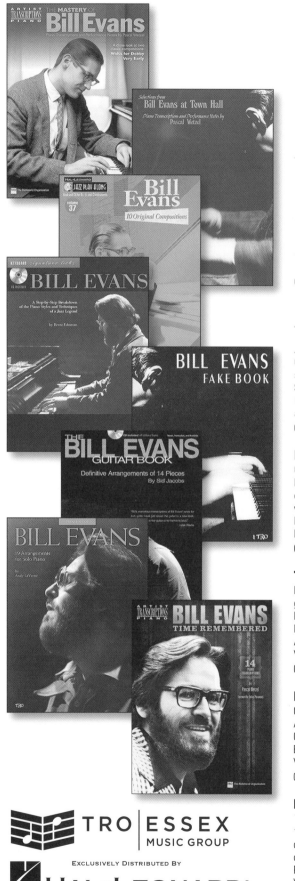

The Mastery of Bill Evans
Piano Transcriptions and Performance Notes by Pascal Wetzel
A close look at two classic compositions: "Waltz for Debby" and "Very Early." Includes both studio and live recording transcriptions, the original piano solo as well as an essay on the evolution of each tune.
00672548 Artist Transcriptions Piano...$12.95

Bill Evans at Town Hall
Piano Transcriptions and Performance Notes by Pascal Wetzel
Recorded live at Town Hall, February 21, 1966: Who Can I Turn To, One for Helen, Solo-In Memory of His Father (including Prologue, Improvisation on Two Themes: Story Line and Turn Out the Stars, and Epilogue). Bonus feature: transcriptions of Only Child and Orbit from "A Simple Matter of Conviction," Funny Man from "Further Conversations with Myself."
00672537 Artist Transcriptions Piano...$16.95

Bill Evans: 10 Original Compositions
Jazz Play-Along Volume 37
Lead sheets with play-along CD for improvisation study and performance. Choice of backing tracks: split track with melody, removable bass and piano; full stereo rhythm section. Funkallero • My Bells • One for Helen • The Opener • Orbit • Show-Type Tune (Tune for a Lyric) • 34 Skidoo • Time Remembered • Turn Out the Stars • Waltz for Debby
00843033 Bb, Eb and C Instrument Books/CD Package...$16.99

Bill Evans – Keyboard Signature Licks
A STEP-BY-STEP BREAKDOWN OF THE PIANO STYLES AND TECHNIQUES OF A JAZZ LEGEND
by Brent Edstrom
An in-depth exploration of the playing style of one of the most influential pianists in jazz. This book/CD pack uses excerpts from a dozen of Evans' best songs to demonstrate his various trademark styles. The CD includes full performance examples, as well as some slowed-down piano solo parts. Songs: Five • One for Helen • The Opener • Peace Piece • Peri's Scope • Quiet Now • Re: Person I Knew • 34 Skidoo • Time Remembered • Turn Out the Stars • Very Early • Waltz for Debby. Includes an introduction by the author.
00695714 Book/CD Pack $22.95

Bill Evans Fake Book – 2nd Edition
60 original compositions transcribed and edited by Pascal Wetzel. Leadsheets generally follow the latest recording to show the evolution of the tune and maturation of the artist. Counterlines, codas, chord extensions and chord changes for improvisation are included. Added features are lyric versions of 10 tunes, 3 essays about Bill Evans' life and music, photographs, and a discography. Includes: Five • Interplay • Laurie • My Bells • Re: The Person I Knew • The Two Lonely People • Time Remembered • Turn Out the Stars • Very Early • Waltz for Debby • and more.
00378800 Melody/Lyrics/Chords $27.50

The Bill Evans Guitar Book
In this book/CD pack, Sid Jacobs translates the playing of quintessential jazz pianist Bill Evans for guitarists to enjoy. Includes music, instruction and analysis of 14 Evans pieces, all in their original keys and with full demonstration tracks on the accompaniment CD. Songs include: Funkallero • Laurie • Letter to Evan • My Bells • Orbit • Peace Piece • Peri's Scope • Remembering the Rain • A Simple Matter of Conviction • Time Remembered • Turn Out the Stars • The Two Lonely People • Very Early • Waltz for Debby.
00699274 Book/CD Pack $19.95

Bill Evans – 19 Arrangements for Solo Piano
Classic Evans compositions simplified and adapted by internationally respected jazz pianist/educator Andy LaVerne, himself a student of Evans. Titles include: Bill's Hit Tune • Laurie • Letter to Evan • One for Helen • Only Child • Orbit • Show-Type Tune (Tune for a Lyric) • Time Remembered • Very Early • Walkin' Up • Waltz for Debby • Your Story • and more. Also includes a reminiscence by LaVerne, with notes on his adaptations.
00000116 Piano Solo $14.95

Bill Evans – Time Remembered
Transcriptions by Pascal Wetzel
14 new transcriptions of Bill Evans' tunes are included in this collection, representing an overview of Evans' career. Features transcriptions by Pascal Wetzel and a foreword by Enrico Pieranunzi. Includes: B Minor Waltz • Fun Ride • Funkallero • Maxine • My Bells • Quiet Now • Remembering the Rain • Since We Met • Song for Helen • 34 Skidoo • Time Remembered • The Two Lonely People • We Will Meet Again • Your Story.
00121885 Piano Transcriptions $19.99

TRO ESSEX MUSIC GROUP

EXCLUSIVELY DISTRIBUTED BY

HAL•LEONARD®

7777 W. BLUEMOUND RD. P.O. BOX 13819 MILWAUKEE, WI 53213

0216